Praise for Make Things in America

Kirkus Reviews. Awards and Accolades: OUR VERDICT √ GET IT

... Olsen lucidly proposes a sweeping tax reform plan and suggests adopting a single-payer national health care plan and a 'Child Sustenance Assistance Service.' The money to pay for these programs and tax cuts will come from taxing stock market and real estate speculation, the latter of which, according to the author, not only artificially raises housing prices but also destabilizes communities (these are provocative points argued with impressive analytical rigor).

...At the heart of the book is a stirring paean to the nobility of work ... "A foundational principle of America is that the economy's very purpose is to serve the needs and aspirations of the American workforce."

...This is a very brief book ... and such a brief treatment of so many complex issues can't be decisively persuasive.

For all its limitations, a worthwhile contribution to an important discussion." — *Kirkus Reviews.*

Readers' Favorite ☆ ☆ ☆ ☆ ☆

...Olsen presents a thoroughly researched argument for diminishing the tax burden on workers and employers to boost productivity and competitiveness in the global market.

...James R. Olsen presents complex economic concepts with detailed analysis and clarity. He supports his arguments with extensive data.

...Make Things in America is a must-read for policymakers, economic students, and anyone interested in understanding and resolving the economic challenges facing the United States today. — *Reviewed by Carol Thompson for Readers' Favorite*

Also by James R. Olsen

I Ching of a Thousand Doors

Hazel's Great Adventure

Covid Wars (publication date May 2025)

MAKE THINGS IN AMERICA

How tax reform can reduce the tax burden on American Workers.

James R. Olsen

AMERICAN REPUBLIC MONOGRAPHS
A MONOGRAPH ON THE AMERICAN WORKER

Breaking Wave Publishing
Hamilton, Montana

Copyright © 2024 James R. Olsen
All Rights Reserved.

No part of this publication may be reproduced, stored in a retrieval system, or transmitted in any form or by any means — electronic, mechanical, photocopy, recording, or otherwise — without prior written permission from the author, except for the inclusion of brief quotes for review for which attribution shall be required.

Moral rights of the authors and artists have been asserted.

No AI Training. This copy is provided solely to be read or listened to by human beings. Among the rights reserved is any right to transmit to or present this work in whole or in part by any means to any artificial intelligence system and/or any automated or semiautomated transformation of this work by itself or in combination with other works. NO AI TRAINING: Without in any way limiting the author's exclusive rights under copyright, any use of this publication to "train" generative artificial intelligence (AI) technologies to generate text is expressly prohibited. The author reserves all rights to license uses of this work for generative AI training and development of machine learning language models.

No Artificial Intelligence (AI) generated content. No text in this book is AI-generated. Software assisted in the editing through spell check, thesaurus, grammar checks, and suggested corrections. No artwork by author is AI generated. The book includes licensed artwork. No AI artwork was sought and the artwork in this book is believed to be solely the work of the artist, though this cannot be guaranteed.

This book is may have errors. The author and publisher no representations or warranties with respect to the accuracy or completeness of the contents of this book and specifically disclaim any implied warranties of merchantability or fitness for a particular purpose.

Photos and artwork have embedded credits. Those not credited to James R. Olsen are licensed through Shutterstock.com, except for the *USNS Observation Island* on page viii, which is a creative commons license from Flicker.com and Endnote 1, which has an insert from the National Archives.

www.JamesROlsen.com

Library of Congress Control Number: 2024926710.
Olsen, James R.
Make Things in America
Illustrated by James R. Olsen

Includes Bibliography and Index
ISBN: 978-1-7342332-5-4

Cover by James R. Olsen
Photo of woodworker by Everyone Photo (License through Shutterstock. Texture, clip, stretch by James R. Olsen)

Dedicated to great bosses
Jane and Steve Odanovich
Constantin (Con) Tsaconas
Colonel Gingrich
Tom O'Mahony
Jack Kelble

Contents

Preface 1

Executive Summary 5

1. Pride in Work 7

2. It's the Real Economy Stupid 11

3. Profit 19

4. Wealth and Excess Wealth 23

5. The National Poker Game 27

6. The Tax-Free Worker 31

7. Raising Children 45

8. How Real Estate Causes the Housing Crisis 53

9. A Fox Guarding Healthcare 59

10. Wants To Work But Can't 71

11. Wasted Energy, Missing Jobs 79

12. The American Worker 91

Endnotes 95

References 105

Index 123

About the Author 129

Photo by Viper-zero. Cropped, touched up, black and white, texture James R. Olsen

Preface

I was an engineer and manager for large defense programs, developing systems where you start with a pile of paper and deliver a system to operators. These included aircraft, ships, ground vehicles, mobile command centers, and buildings that host a lot of mission systems complete with electronics and software. When the pieces are put together, there are always a few problems whose cause you just cannot put your finger on.

Of course, there were hundreds of other problems the team could work on, so there was a choice. One is to do the hard work on the hard problems now. Or, put it off, working on the easy issues while applying band-aids to hard ones. This way, you can report great progress.

Of course, the thing about these systems is that you cannot, not finish. As the punch list gets small, there are still the hard problems that were put off until later. Now, more than band-aids are needed. You can't fake it because, as we used to say, physics gets the last vote. So now the team slogs through the hard problems, month after month.

Only a few percent of these programs are on time and on budget (Hofbauer 2011, Erwin 2024). At some point, you have to figure it out. If you want to be one of the few who delivers the goods on time and on budget, you work on the hard problems earlier rather than later — do the right thing now.

We know in our hearts that an economy that only provides services will not work. We need to make more of our own things. It is a hard problem. The American economy has managed to lose much of its manufacturing prowess. Too often, our politicians, with great fanfare, put band-aids on it.

Make Things in America Again

Photo by Everyone Photo Textured Black and White by James R Olsen

Photo by Master1305 Texturized converted to Black and White by James R Olsen

When are we going to do the right thing for our economy?

If we do business as usual, the band-aids will keep falling away; manufacturing, healthy farms, and a prosperous workforce will bleed away. This monograph proposes doing the right thing for the American Worker. It begins with the worker and the household budget — the worker's view. The result is tax reform that fixes the household budget. It will go a long way to fixing our economy and lifting everyone.

James R. Olsen
Hamilton, Montana, October 11, 2024

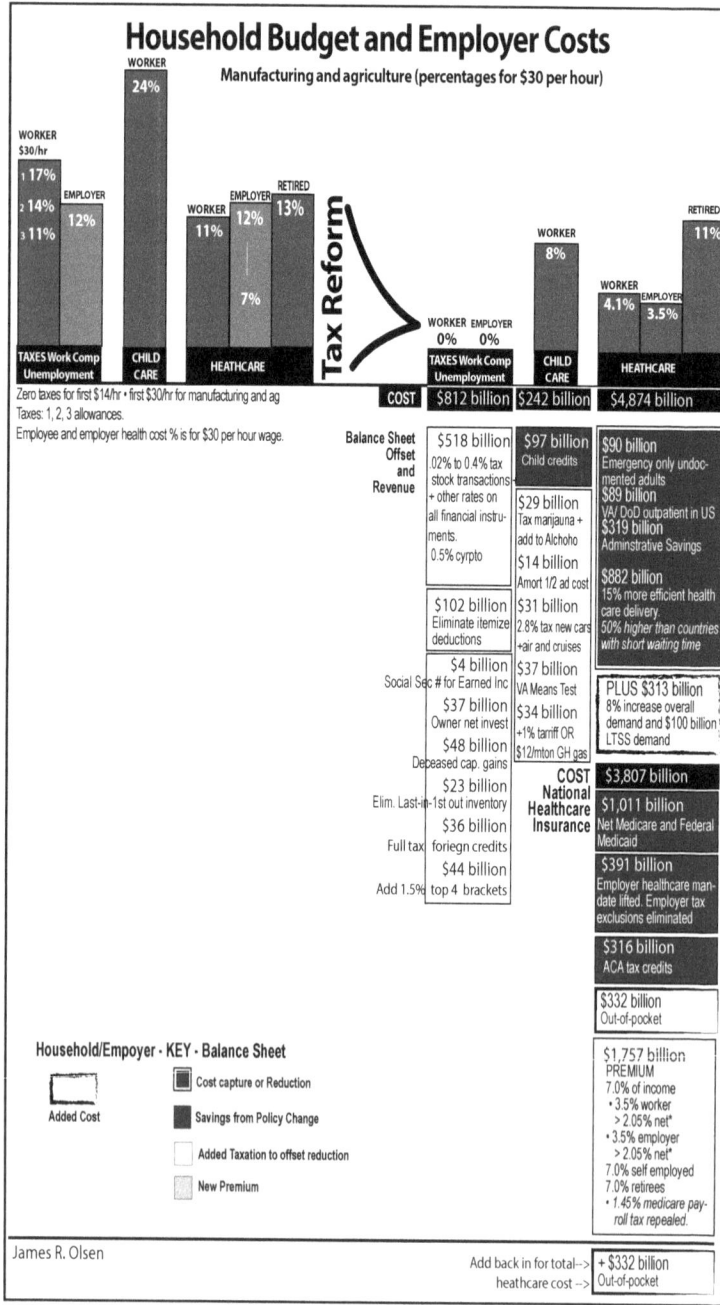

Executive Summary

Make Things in America shows how to make capitalism work for workers. It begins with the nature of the economy — working in the household is part of the "real" economy. Using government estimates, a tax reform emerges that makes American Workers more productive:

- Implement a tax-neutral plan that eliminates the income tax and Social Security tax burden for the worker and employer for the first $14 per hour and the first $30 an hour for manufacturing and agriculture.
- Provide Child Sustenance payments for every child in America with a plan that recognizes the value of work in the household. The proposal covers 80% of the average childcare cost for working people making less than $50,000 per year and 65% for stay-at-home parents — 67% up to $100,000 a year, 50% up to $200,000 a year, and help over that.
- Tax real estate to favor primary residences and rentals and slow speculation with transfer taxes.
- Dramatically lower healthcare costs with the most effective system: a national health plan paid for with a premium of 3.5% of income, matched by the employer, halving the average family's and employer's cost.

Trust accounts with annual adjustments to tax rates and tax relief, child sustenance, and national healthcare makes these plans self-funding without needing to find additional funding for estimate errors or changes in cash flow.

With this as a basis, people can be brought out of poverty by reforming housing vouchers, simplifying poverty support, and supporting transition into the workforce.

Supply-side, trickle-down economics has been tried for decades. Even so, manufacturing jobs left America and the national deficit has grown. It is time to implement the trickle-up effect of a more productive American Worker.

• 1 •

PRIDE IN WORK

Nobility can be found in work, from sweeping floors to running a business, from raising children to being a pediatric doctor, from planting crops to running a grocery store, from deckhand to ship captain, from programmer to tech entrepreneur, from first-grade teacher to university professor, from nurse to chief of medicine, from walking a beat to chief of police, from city clerk to mayor, from social worker to psychiatrist, from postal carrier to President. The nobility lies in a job that contributes to society and is a job well done.

> When I was coming up, my folks weren't poor; my folks weren't rich. My mother's brother had graduated from college — he was the only one I knew of all of my ancestors. Indeed, on my father's side, it was a family of farmers, laborers, and skilled workers. With the coming of World War II, my father and several brothers of fighting age were soldiers and naval aviators.
>
> My father was the naval aviator in the family. The first thing I could remember him telling me was that I was going to college. But, by the time I reached high school, my father, reaching back to his working-class heritage, insisted I needed to make a living by the time I was 18. I did both.
>
> I started working with adult crews when I was 16, after school and summers. I worked as a grocery bagger in the commissary on the base. We didn't get paid; we only got tips. I got good at it. A tip was most often paid after packing the grocery bags, tak-

ing them to the car, and putting them in. 25¢ or 35¢ was the expected reward for two, three, or four bags.

Not every "bag boy" did well. But, if I stayed on my feet for four to six hours straight and ran back from the car with the grocery cart to get back in line for the next customer quickly, I averaged 150% of minimum wage. When things were slow, and we weren't having the "oldest coin" contest, we would sometimes see who was the fastest. Two paper bags, double-bagged, packed with groceries, being swept with a backhand by the grocery checker as the cash register clicked the prices onto a paper tape, bags filled just right, not too heavy, light stuff on the top—time: Twenty-eight seconds. I took pride in doing this job well.

Over the next six years, I learned more. At a DQ, I learned to be a server and fry cook; at a lumber yard, I swept floors, cut custom orders, drove a flatbed, tied a load, custom-cut wood, cut glass, keyed locks, hung doors, moved loads with a forklift, sorted and graded lumber, balanced the cash register; on a summer trip south, I pumped gas, washed windshields, checked the oil and tire pressure; I worked as a painter's helper just long enough to be a decent house painter to then bid on some painting jobs; I partnered up with a retired Navy Chief Petty Officer to build residential fences; and day-labor could be almost anything that involves putting your back into it. Learning to do these jobs well was rewarding. I still put these six years on my resumé. Doing them well was as satisfying as running large, complex engineering development programs for defense and air traffic control — I also spent years learning how to do that well.

1. Pride in Work

Work is part of the human condition. To be good at something is rewarding. Of course, some work is not so good — a bad boss, dangerous working conditions — dipping galvanized metal with my greased hands and forearms into solvents on mid-shift in a paint shop. Even though it paid well, I quit that job after three shifts.

On the other hand, too much leisure is not suitable for most people (Sharif 2021). Work is a factor in the self-esteem equation (Gómez-Jorge 2023, Griffen 1996), though the whole history of biology, family, and experience goes into self-esteem — and there is a library full of books on the subject. Whether a person has work can be critical to someone who does not already enjoy high self-esteem (Shamir 1986).

The bottom line is that members of a society provide goods and services to each other. A worthwhile aspiration is rewarding work, whether for pay, self-employment, volunteering, or participation in the household. There are exceptions, but work usually contributes to society, which is also a worthwhile aspiration.

Unfortunately, we don't recognize all work when discussing our economy — unpaid work in the household.

Photo by Tiplyashina Evgeniya, Cropped, black and white, texture by James R. Olsen

· 2 ·
IT'S THE REAL ECONOMY STUPID

A sign installed by James Carville at Bill Clinton's campaign headquarters said, "It's the economy stupid." As we watch manufacturing flee from our shores, it's still the economy.

We must look at our economy and how we value work to see why. What is an economy?

It can be seen as society's marketplace. "Biological markets are all over the place," says Ronald Noë, a Dutch biologist at the University of Strasbourg who first proposed the concept of the biological market in 1994 (Crair 2017, Noë 1994). An alpha male baboon will allow a beta male to use some of its territory if it cares for the baby baboons. A cleaner wrasse eats parasites off other fish, often much bigger fish — but the bigger fish don't eat them because they are getting parasites picked off its skin, Sometimes the wrasse will take a nip of flesh along with it. If there is another cleaning station nearby that the big client fish could visit, the cleaner wrasse will behave more gently. Nature is full of market economies.

If the jungle were made up of always-selfish individuals who never cooperated, never helped another individual, and always tried to fool every other individual, the proverbial lion would be one big, fat king of the jungle who had eaten everything else, only to look across the empty savanna and realize it was going to starve to death. Likewise, the idea that a real-life human economy is made up of individuals who are only driven by selfishness in a free-trade free-for-all is a construct that fails society and doesn't exist in the real world (Riis 1890, Keynes 1933).

The Britannica Dictionary defines economy as:

> The process or system by which goods and services are produced, sold, and bought in a country or region.

This definition and others like it have the circulation of money as central to their definition. But humans have been around for a long time and have engaged in economic activity before money. Let's take "bought and sold" out of the definition to define our economy:

> The process by which a society provides goods and services to each other.

This definition serves for societies ranging from small hunter-gatherer tribes to the Roman Empire to the rise of capitalism, to a Bolshevik command economy, to the Chinese move to managed capitalism, to what we call democracies — various versions of Republics with various mixtures of socialism and capitalism.

The Utopian aspirations of Karl Marx's communism and Adam Smith's free market capitalism are too mechanistic. There is a human element. Neither was ever fulfilled because, in practice, the dictatorship of the proletariat fell to power-hungry party leaders. The corporate mandate to maximize profits fell to Judeo-Christian and humanist ethics, which could not abide children starving on the streets, chained to coal carts, tending motor-driven looms, five-year-olds of all races picking cotton for pay, or dying at the doors of the emergency room because the parents could not pay. (Riis 1890, National Child Labor Committee Collection 1904, Baker 2024).

This dry definition begs the question: What is the purpose of a society providing goods and services? Who is it for? In the United States, we have only to look at our founding documents, which declare that all people are created equal — our national aspiration is that everyone has an equal opportunity. So, the purpose of the American economy is to serve the people in society. So, let's expand our definition:

> The process by which a society provides goods and services for individuals and society as a whole.
>
> *Or, more to the point (remembering that "work" includes unpaid activities in the household):*
>
> The American economy is the process by which a society provides goods and services for American Workers and society as a whole.

For the libertarian or never-socialist crowd who worries over "society as a whole," I mention roads and rails in America. Travel down the Eastern seaboard during the American Revolution involved a series of privately owned turnpikes — most of whom lost money but were financed by local business owners because they knew if you built it, trade would come. President Thomas Jefferson was the one who started the federal government in the business of road building, a road through the Cumberland Gap. (Bahadori 2008, Kien 2008). Let's not forget the Railroad Barons, owners of private companies that received generous land grants and federal support to build transcontinental railroads.

So, while there are plenty of economic theories, any theory that does not serve the American Worker is flawed "by definition."

The economy definition we have here applies to a tribe moving across the plains, practicing this provision of goods and services for the individuals in the tribe and the tribal society as a whole, with no need for money, as they gather food, hunt for food, prepare food, make clothing, build housing, keep living spaces warm in the winter, transport food and goods, heal the sick, teach children, provide entertainment, and train warriors for the common defense. This "work," and who does it, is driven by cultural customs.

When the tribe met another person from another tribe, they might trade. They might trade one valuable item for another. More active trading occurred if there was a rendezvous at a particular time of year when tribes met to share stories and trade.

There is little in this economy that does not happen in some form in our modern economy. Our tribe has a Real Domestic Product, which consists of all of the goods and services the tribal members provide for each other and trade with other tribes. How does our Real Domestic Product (RDP) compare to our government's calculation of the Gross Domestic Product (GDP), a number that is watched closely and touted widely if it goes up? (Ferando-1 2024, Wikipedia "Gross Domestic Product").

GDP for a nation is the sum of its people's productivity to create monetary (paid for with money) goods and services. The United States leads the world in GDP. However, when divided by the population to get per capita (per person) GDP, some smaller countries do better: Luxembourg, Singapore, Ireland, Norway, Qatar, United Arab Republics, and Switzerland. China, with the second largest GDP, also has the largest population. On a per capita basis, China comes in 72nd after Mexico. (Worldometer 2024). However, China leads the world in manufacturing, making 31% of the world's products compared to 12% for the United States. (Safeguard Global 2024).

When we include non-monetized goods and services in our RDP, we find that RDP is greater than GDP. Here is the formula of GDP used by the government:

GDP = Consumer Spending [C] + Investment [I] + Government Spending [G] + (Exports – Imports)

What GDP does not include are goods and services that are provided but not sold — that is, Non-Monetary Trans-

actions — things such as parental childcare, labor for do-it-yourself repairs, home food preparation, and food products from a garden or farm eaten at home. And, of course, the GDP does not account for products and services traded in informal markets or on the black market. Let's split Non-Monetary Transactions into those primarily in the home:
1) Household Domestic Product (HDP)
2) Informal:
    a) Black markets (usually illegal products and services),
    b) Unmeasured Domestic Product (UDP).

RDP = GDP + HDP + UDP + Black Markets

Unmeasured Domestic Product (UDP) includes volunteer work, bartering, the ubiquitous points system used by credit cards, airlines, and hotel chains, and small-scale transactions between individuals and street markets. While volunteer work is not measured, surveys and estimates estimate that it amounts to $135 to $225 billion annually (Pho 2004). Some barter is accounted for when reported to the IRS, but much isn't. It is hard to estimate, with one source suggesting $12 to $14 billion (IRTA 2024). Points for airline credit cards are worth about $23 billion a year (Airlines of America 2022). Add another $23 billion if 10% of tips go unreported to the IRS (Weir 2018). To give a sense of proportion, 1% of the monetary GDP measured by the government is $250 billion.

Look at HDP, Household Domestic Product, after World War II. In the '50s and '60s, there was a tremendous rise in the Ad Men peddling labor-saving devices to homemakers and things like the best car ever to men (Warren 1997 p.6, Berry 1977 p.119, Mad Men 2007). The percentage of two-income households went from 23% to 39%, even as male wages rose. In the late '60s and '70s, the feminist movement and equal-pay-for-equal-work resulted in more workplace opportunities for women.

Even so, there is still a small percentage shortfall in equal-pay-for-equal-work. However, an important confounding factor is that equal-pay-for-equal-work is not necessarily equal-pay-for-equal-value. A female-dominant profession may have the same value for society as a male-dominated profession, but the market wages differ. The median salary for all work for women working full time is lower than for males, though the difference has gotten smaller, going from 60¢ to the dollar to 84¢ to the dollar. (Daughtery 2024, Data Team Economist 2017).

What is going on in the real economy? What happened post-World War II were an ad campaigns that denigrated the frugal householder, even while many women had aspirations for a professional career; the former is destructive, the latter is admirable. The economic result is that much of household non-monetary economics got replaced with the need for more cash to pay for "labor-saving devices" in the home and for childcare outside the home.

Because the GDP looks only at the money, the computed domestic product doesn't include household economics. It does not discount the increasing cost of housing – housing which may cost more but has the same economic utility to the householder no matter what it costs.

These two factors alone suggest that the GDP per capita rise from about in 2024 dollars from $12,000 post World War II to $68,000 may be a false narrative. Are we are 4 or 5 times better off? Since 1953, the median income for a family has improved 2.3 times, but since the 1970s, the middle class has shrunk by over 10%. And the rich got richer. (FRED-2 2023, Kochhar 2024). Are we 2.3 times off?

A house is a house is a house. A house is the most significant investment for most families, and they have become more expensive. For a decade and a half after World War II,

2. It's the Real Economy Stupid

this number grew so that by the 1960s, the price of a house was 4 to 5 annual household incomes. It is now 7.5 times the annual household income. (Long Term Trends 2024). Are we that much better off?

We have been talking about the United States as a whole, but these numbers are not evenly divided by ethnicity or gender. There remain significant gaps. Our Gross Domestic Product math and post-war economic tour are the first steps in a tax plan to reduce the tax burden on the American real economy.

We described our economy as the actual exchange of goods and services. So far, we have constructed an economy that could be capitalist, socialist, mercantile, or the empire model used by Ancient Rome. If the "someone" who owns capital is the State, we could be close to the communist economic model.

However, implementing each of these models has resulted in an unequal distribution of wealth. The question is, how did it get that way? We leave the rest behind and deal with the American version of capitalism — which, in reality, is a capitalist system with socialist underpinnings established over time beginning in the late nineteenth and early twentieth century.

Photo by PeopleImages.com black and white texture by James B. Dixon

· 3 ·

PROFIT

A craftsperson has a small shop that contains the tools of their trade. With their own hands, they make something, say well-crafted beautiful wooden chairs. Of course, this craftsperson must buy the wood, pay rent for the shop, etc. If the craftsperson makes eight chairs daily, working 200 days during the year and selling them for $50 each, customers pay $100,000. The material, rent, and everything else needed to make the chairs cost $20,000.

> Profit = Total Revenue – Total Expenses = $80,000.

Our craftsperson's profit is our craftsperson's wages. Our craftsperson has managed to make more than the median wage in the United States. The following year, our craftsperson hires another person for $80,000, and the two of them make sixteen chairs a day and earned $200,000 in revenue. But, while the material cost will double, the rent stays the same. So let's say the expenses are not 2 x $20,000 but $30,000. The total expenses now include our new helper's wages of $80,000.

> Total Expenses = $30,000 for expenses + $80,000 helper's wages = $110,000
>
> Profit = Total Revenue - $110,000 = $90,000.

By taking the risk of promising wages and assuming that the revenue would cover those wages, our craftsperson has made more profit, earning a raise. But our craftsperson could have made less money if the sales had fallen short.

This seems fair enough. Our craftsperson has only used their own money. Let's call this Owner-Worker-Profit, which, in all fairness, is equivalent to wages.

Years go by, and our craftsperson wants to retire and meets a capitalist willing to buy the company and the designs in return for a nice retirement account. The deal is done.

Our capitalist, however, does not go to work building chairs. Instead, our capitalist writes a business plan and gets a hundred people to invest. Of course, the investors want a share of the profits. And since their money will be used to build a small factory, they want to share ownership—after all, it is their money being put up. If the business fails, they will lose their money.

Since the investors want to invest different amounts, stock certificates are issued, showing the share of the company the investor now owns. Our capitalist sees that the artisan's work can be broken into twelve steps, and, with some machines, six of those steps can be automated. So, the investor's money is used to build a factory and hire workers to producing 1,000 chairs a day.

Since we now have many workers, some managers will be hired. Since the workers do not need to be as skilled as our craftsperson, a $64,000-a-year wage is enough to attract the talent required. The profit is calculated and, after putting some aside for future investments and cash flow, distributed to the investors in proportion to how much each invested — a dividend.

Since the investors aren't working making chairs, their investment is a matter of how much return on investment they will get. Of course, if the expected return is not more than the interest on a certificate of deposit, it would make no sense for them to invest.

The investors did not just buy the company but invested in capital to make more chairs-per-person-day. The investors would make more money if the company sold many more chairs. Even so, things could have gone wrong: What if they could not sell that many more chairs? What if the equipment broke down too often? What if the wages they planned weren't sufficient to attract workers? The investors took risks with their money. Here, the profit is not equivalent to wages but is a return on investment, an investment that involves a risk of loss. Welcome to capitalism.

Capitalism in this "pure" form depends on a fair and equitable marketplace. But, from its very beginning, the manipulation by big business for unfair advantages began — monopolies and trusts; low wages, long hours, and dangerous working conditions for desperate families displaced by mechanization in the countryside; big money buying an unleveled playing field from politicians — and thus we got labor laws, regulations, and trust-busting Presidents. There is a library full of books on this, so we'll leave it there.

Next, we turn to wealth. Looking at the wealth from a working-class neighborhood, we see half the people in the United States hold only 2.5% of the nation's wealth, while 10% of the people in the United States hold 68% percent of the wealth, and 1 in 1,000 people hold 14% of the wealth. The 400 richest (0.00013% of the population) have 3.2% of the wealth. (Stastica 2024, USA Facts-1 2023, LaFranco 2024). We'll talk about the various ways wealth is generated and look at the very uneven distribution of wealth.

Make Things in America Again

Photo by aastcok. Clip black amd white texture James R. Olsen

· 4 ·
WEALTH AND EXCESS WEALTH

So far, the economy described is for products and services put to use. But in our tribal trading camp, a horse is something everyone knows can be traded for many other things. If someone accumulated a string of eight horses when they were only using two or three for their family, the remaining horses are wealth.

But, since the dictionary definition of "wealth" is all the goods owned, even those used to live and work, we could define the string of horses as "Excess Wealth," wealth not needed immediately for real economic activity. But an extra horse or two could be required if a horse died or went lame. So, let's define Excess Wealth as wealth beyond that which is needed now and in the foreseeable future to participate in real economic activity. This has a bit of subjectivity, but it will help in the forthcoming discussion.

Someone owns a company that makes bricks. They buy materials, hire wage earners, and make a thousand bricks. That someone now owns a pile of thousand bricks. The bricks, the product of economic activity, now rest in storage, a storage bin of economic activity. They are "worth" something. They "cost" the labor and materials to make them. They are worth what someone will "pay" for them — wealth. The bricks sit there month after month. Food is grown, prepared, and eaten; things are made and sold; buildings are built. The pile of bricks sits there, watching the economy go by.

Then, one day, a builder buys the bricks. Off they go to a building site for a brick wall, becoming part of that economic activity. Now, the brick wall costs the sum of the cost of the bricks and the other materials and labor to build it. While it is once again "wealth," it also participates in economic activity, such as a wall in a building or a building that serves the economy.

A worker who made the bricks may take some of their pay, the fruits of their labor, and put it in a savings account. This becomes a storage place for the fruits of their labor — their savings — wealth. Our worker may want an inflation hedge and buy gold or get a little more interest for their money and buy a bond — that is, lending their money to the government or a business — wealth.

When our craftsperson sold the business to our capitalist, the capitalist raised money by selling company shares and providing stock certificates as evidence of ownership of a transaction of the company. The stocks have value; they are wealth. They can be bought and sold. So, if all of a company's assets, the buildings, machinery, inventory, and materials, are worth $10 million and there are 100,000 shares of stock, each share would be worth $100 if the company were liquidated. However, the company is expected to make a profit of $1 million this year. If the stock price is $100, the company has what is called a price/earnings ratio (P/E) of 10. Six months later, as everyone sees the profit heading to a million by year's end, our shareholder can probably find a buyer for more than $100.

The furniture industry is growing, and our chair company's innovations and style are taking the industry by storm; we expect profits to grow to 25%. A P/E of 20 seems justified, and everyone is confident about the future, so why wait? People who believe in that future will pay for it. Our shareholders now have stock worth $200.

As the year ends, the million in profit is delivered and sales increase — and 25% for next year is assured. So, why

4. Wealth and Excess Wealth

wait? People are willing to buy a share for $450. Since stocks are wealth, our shareholders have increased their wealth. If a stockholder sells their shares, they make money; it is a gain in the price of their share of the capital, called "capital gains."

It is essential to realize that even as the share prices rise and stockholders sell shares, none of this money goes into the company's treasury. The company may issue more shares and get in on the action, but now there are more total shares. If the company issues another 100,000 shares of our chair company stock, the existing shareholders own less of the company by half. Their stock has been "diluted." They may not like that, and the owners of 51% of the company may not allow it.

Oh no, a new chair company comes roaring in. The competition is stiff. The 25% growth in profit disappears; The people who paid $450 lament as the share price falls back to $200. And so goes the stock market.

Let's say our craftsperson was not ready to retire but wanted to grow the company. So, the craftsperson forms a corporation. The craftsperson will own all of the stock. However, the corporation then issues more stock and sells it to investors. The company grows and becomes more profitable. The stock price goes up and up. The craftsperson's stock is now worth more. We now have a craftsperson with more wealth.

When we say capitalism stimulates innovation, this is often how it works. The company grows, helping the economy grow, and the owners' wealth grows. Some get rich.

This is an "Investment."

Our economy is more complex than our story of creating wealth by working and investing to build a business. There are other ways people get rich — pure speculation.

Make Things in America Again

Photo by Grenhoff, black and white, fade background by James R. Olsen

· 5 ·
THE NATIONAL POKER GAME

Poker is entertainment. Poker is also a zero-sum game: The total amount of money on the table is the same as when the players started; when someone wins, someone loses. The real economy that provides useful goods and services is not zero-sum. Everyone wins as they provide valuable goods and services to each other. Henry Ford invented the production line, a more efficient way of making cars. He paid double the going wage for workers and produced affordable cars that cost less — very beneficial to the real economy (Neilson 2005).

However, what does the money transferred between winners and losers in a poker game add to the economy? — zero. In fact, for the real economy, a high-stakes poker game could be a negative drag on the real economy. Say a player wins big, accumulating excess wealth. Granted, this wealth could be invested, but it could buy a bigger, shinier car. Nevertheless, there are losers. The real economy suffers if a player loses so much that they can't make the rent.

The stock market began as investing. Buying stocks based on a company's value and actual earnings is investing. The companies in the stock market will, on average, increase the amount of goods and services they produce, sometimes with growing profits; all the boats are lifted with the rising tide.

Stock investments are a bet on the future of the company. A stock will sell for more if a buyer thinks earnings will increase. It is investing because the bet is on the company (Campbell 2024).

There are those who trade stocks but are not to invest. They speculate. They do not bet on a company's future; instead, they bet on what the other people trading in the market will do. They are playing poker. We are not going to go into the myriad ways to play the stock market without investing in a stock for the long run, mostly legal: day trading, margin buys, options, stock futures, short-squeeze, derivatives, and some not: pump-and-dump, poop-and-scoop, and the list goes on.

We must be careful here because it depends on what people are speculating about. An early long-term buyer of Tesla or Nvidia speculated that the company would do well, even if other potential investors were not so sure. An early long-term buyer of Tesla or Nvidia was buying stock because they thought there was a better chance of the company growing fast than failing.

Some professionals see speculation as adding more "liquidity," a ready buyer and seller in a market. But then, there is the speculator who is not betting on the company but on the crowd and the price movements from day to day (Wikipedia. "Speculation"). Let's give this a special name, "pure speculation," a term used in 1902 because this is the speculation we would rather tax (Ryan 1902).

The stock market crash of 1929 was driven by pure speculation. Many stocks kept increasing at an unprecedented rates as more people poured their savings into the market; people bought on margin to make a quick buck. "Margin" means that the stock buyer only puts up a portion of the price, 10%, and the rest is borrowed. If the stock price drops 10%, the lender calls in the loan, the stock is sold and the buyer loses all their money — and it finally happened. On October 28,

1929 stocks fell 13% and panic set in. An even bigger one-day percentage drop in the stock market occurred in 1987 on Black Monday when a bubble burst (Federal Reserve History 2024, Wikipedia "Black Monday").

Stock market pure speculation periodically creates busts: the 2000 dotcom bust (Wikipedia "Dot.com bubble") and the 2010 crash, driven by auto-trading computer software feeding on each other faster than humans could react (Wikipedia "2010 flash crash"). Pure speculation is, at best, a worthless economic activity; at worst, it damages our economy and reduces society's overall wealth. Speculators may "follow the rules," but their winnings are excess wealth won at the expense of others.

If wages and investment support the real economy and pure speculation hurts it, which should we tax? We can level the playing field between speculators and working people by taxing pure speculation more and taxing wages less in equal amounts.

• 6 •
THE TAX-FREE WORKER

The United States Supreme Court ruled that the tax scheme that Abraham Lincoln used to finance the Civil War was unconstitutional. The 16th Amendment was a rebuttal; it made Lincoln's tax legal. When Wyoming ratified the Amendment on February 3, 1913, the United States embarked on a radical tax reform — the income tax (IRS-3 2024). Until then, the country had supported itself with excise taxes on imports and things like alcoholic beverages. A century later, we find ourselves with a heavily tax-burdened worker, a worker who is the backbone of our economy.[1] It is time for tax reform that removes this burden.

The productivity of the American Worker is often touted as one of the best (Lahart 2025). So, why have manufacturing jobs moved to China? How productivity is calculated hides why manufacturing jobs migrate to places like China. At a national level, the GDP is divided by labor hours. The equation used by the government to compute the productivity of the American Worker looks at their hours worked as a commodity:

Productivity = GDP ÷ Total Hours Worked

For a business, productivity is often defined as the product's value divided by hours of labor. Yet, if we reduce the cost of an hour of labor, the calculated productivity will not change, even though it will cost less to produce products. We measure worker Value-Added-per-Worker, but don't seem to include it in productivity (BLS-11 2024, Liberman 2008).

The cost of an hour of labor is essential. An additional is informative — the product's value divided by the cost of labor, including taxes:

> Real Labor Productivity = GDP ÷ Cost of Labor
>
> In terms of other metrics the government uses:
> = GDP ÷ (Total Hours Worked x Ave Hourly Labor Cost)
> = Value-Added-per-Worker x Ave Hrs per Worker per Yr ÷ Ave Hourly Labor Cost

If Hourly Labor Cost is reduced by eliminating payroll taxes, Real Labor Productivity goes up — and it will with what I am proposing.

A significant factor in the calculation of productivity is the leverage of capital. Henry Ford's production line increased productivity. When Elon Musk bought a mold to make a Tesla car body, he increased Tesla's productivity. (Kenton 2024, Cantrell 2024, Chew 2012). But, compare a line worker at a factory with a person pushing buttons to mold a car body — are the workers themselves suddenly better workers? No. Tesla is more productive because the company needs fewer working hours to make a car body.

As far as the economy is concerned, those workers Elon did not need to hire have to find jobs doing something else. If all goes well, the economy will grow with more businesses hiring those workers. All is not well if jobs disappear during a recession or migrate overseas and Americans cannot find work.

Remember who the economy serves — the purpose of its existence — American Workers and their families. The American Worker's productivity is dragged down by taxes for both workers and the businesses that employ them, making those workers more expensive than they need to be. And this makes American companies less competitive.

The answer for some politicians is that it is a race to get everyone a college degree as if it is a gateway to fully participating in the economy. But, organizing an economy that requires college ignores the Intelligence Quotient (IQ) Bell Curve. People may have intelligence not measured by the IQ test — they may be just as wise and have as much productive potential as those at the top of the IQ Bell Curve. They may be very good at a trade or business savvy. Should a college degree be a prerequisite for a good job? No. The people in America can and should be able to fully participate in the American economy with a fulfilling job without needing a degree.

Given our definition of an economy — people in society providing goods and services for each other and society as a whole — people who can work should work. We can only expect this if we structure our economy so everyone on the Bell Curve can have a fulfilling job — remembering that work in our real economy includes household economics and unpaid work inside the home. How can we create well-paid, fulfilling jobs for everyone in America? One thing we need to do is to bring back manufacturing.

Most low-tech manufacturing has left the United States. China, the latest nation to accelerate large-scale industrialization in the 1980s, has overtaken the United States in manufacturing (Brand 2017, Wikipedia "Manufacturing"). The average manufacturing wage in China is $6.25. (Statista-2 2023). The tax burden for employees and employers in China varies by province but appears higher than in the United States, ranging from 25% to 32% (PriceWaterHouseCopper 2024). This brings Chinese manufacturing labor cost to $8.25 per hour, more than the

U.S. minimum wage. However, American Workers and the businesses that employ them have a tax burden of their own.

And Americans aspire to earn a living wage. A living wage in Montana for a single person is $20 per hour for a single person and $35 for a married couple with one child (Glasmeier 2024). To achieve the aspiration of a living wage for all and a more competitive workforce, we can strip American Workers of their tax burden. If we do this, we will be within shooting distance of competing with the Chinese worker, needing only a factor of two capital leverage for lower-tech manufacturing. It has a better chance of success than a tariff war (Keynes 1933). We can make America more competitive in industries such as clothing (Argyle Hays 2018) and bring jobs back home.

If we go further for selected industries and allow a $20 per hour tax credit for the employer, labor costs will equal the average cost-to-hire manufacturing worker in China. While unaffordable across the board, it could jump-start selected industries.

And, while we're at it, high-tech manufacturing requires both innovative capital leverage and employees with less tax burden — we can innovate to bring high-tech home as well (Beyer 2024. Brandt 2024).

So, let's strip American Workers of some of their tax burden. First, let's focus on the first $14 per hour. Social Security tax, 6.2%, and Medicare, 1.45%, means 7.65% is taken from the wage earner's paycheck. The employer must pay another 7.65%, so the total tax for an hour of work is 15.3%. For the first $14.00 an hour, this is $2.14 per hour. In addition, depending on the family situation and total income, most workers also pay an average income tax of 40¢ per hour when making $14 per hour (ARRP 2024). We can relieve the wage earner and the employer of this tax burden for the first $14 in hourly wage, reducing the worker's annual tax by $2,697 and the employer's tax by $1,963.

America is an economic powerhouse: the total personal income from all sources, wages, self-employment, business, investments, and retirement in the United States is $25.1 trillion. Half of this is wages and salaries (FRED-5 2024, FRED-4 2023).

In 2023, there were 259 billion paid labor hours performed by 168 million workers in the United States (FRED-2 2023, BLS-6 2024). Manufacturing workers number 13 million (BLS-1 2024, BLS-4 2024). The number of workers in agriculture is 3.6 million (USDA 2024). While the average wage is $34 in manufacturing, the middle-class and non-supervisory manufacturing workers average $30 per hour (FRED-3 2024, Nash 2024. BSL-8 2024).

We target manufacturing and agriculture for the first $30 per hour. We can go further by eliminating other employer costs. First is workman's compensation, which varies quite a bit by industry and state, as well as the accident rate. It averages $1.10 an hour for manufacturing. (BLS-7 2024, WorkCompLab 2024). Similarly, unemployment insurance varies by state, industry, and employer experience — we can allocate 1% to cover part of it — 30¢ an hour.

In summary, we have relieved the employee and employer of the tax burden for the first $30 paid for an hour of work for manufacturing and agriculture and the first $14 for all other jobs. We relieved manufacturing and agriculture employers of workman's comp and some or all unemployment insurance.

This tax reform applies to independent contractors, including gig workers and self-employed (though for them, it is called a self-employment tax and is applied to net earnings). Of course, independent contractors will be expected to report and certify hours worked. (Further, Congress should legislate that any company that "captures" freelancers for a large part of the services, such as Uber, make at least minimum wage or pay the difference.)

The tax relief is limited to paid time. For wage earners, it includes paid sick time, holidays, vacation, and family leave. It is limited to full-time hours, which is 2,080 hours a year.

The American Worker tax relief will cost an estimated $814 billion (IRS-1 2024, ARRP 2024, FRED-2 2023, BSL-1 2023).[2] The question is how to pay for it. We will walk through tax reform initiatives to cover this so we end up with a tax-neutral plan.

Imagine we had a trust fund to draw from, but we were unsure if our estimates would cover our goals. If we reserve one-quarter of it to cover the uncertainties, we take the other three-quarters and distribute it hour by hour. We look at every paid hour for a legally eligible worker in the United States (Citizens, Green Card, and Work Permit holders). Of course, the employer will need to keep track and report every paid hour if they want their tax break, which they usually do anyway.

Imagine someone working for $30 an hour and actually getting a paycheck for $30 and costing the employer $30 with no tax strings attached.

This tax reform will help the American Worker and the employer of the American Worker to be more productive and competitive.

NEEDED: $814 billion

It is a lot, but we can get there. To get to a net zero tax impact, let's turn to taxing pure speculation to help pay for it. As I write this, there were over 16 billion stock trades *in one day* (Cboe-1 2024). The total value of stocks traded in 2023 was $128 trillion (CBoe-2 2024). What if we tax these transactions?

Some will say, "Oh no! Taxing transactions will be devastating; it has never been done before." But it has, and it is. As we go through the day, we pay transaction taxes and fees: sales tax, credit card fees paid by the vendor, and gas tax. Transaction taxes and fees burden much of our economy.

Turning to stocks, New York State charges a minuscule stock transaction fee (New York State, Department of Taxation and Finance 2024). Of course, stockbrokers and online brokerages charge a fee to buy and sell a stock. The so-called free online trades are the brokers pocketing the difference between bid-to-ask or kickbacks from market makers for the privilege of sending business their way (Montevigren 2024).

This is not new. Until 1966, the United States had a transaction fee of 0.2% for stock transactions (Wikipedia "Financial Transaction Tax," Miller 2020). It has been discussed in Congress and studied in academia. The market reaction is a worry since increasing the transaction cost may have investors and speculators going elsewhere. People will work around a transaction tax if they can. Thus, any transfer tax must apply to all financial instruments.

Some have proposed transaction taxes as high as 0.5% (Senate Bill 1587 116th Congress 2019, Wikipedia, "Financial Transaction Tax"). When the Congressional Budget Office (CBO) studied a 0.01% to 0.1% tax on transactions, they predicted that rapid trades, mainly pure speculation, would be severely curtailed. At the same time, long-term investors will easily bear the difference — yes, the tax will reduce the asset's value, but the amount is less than a week of the average price change for most publicly traded stocks (Financial Samurai 2024).

Proposals suggest different rates for different financial transactions, such as stocks, bonds, derivatives, and treasury notes, to minimize the tax distorting how the market works — except for reducing the incentive for short-term speculation (CBO-3 2019 Option 37 p. 298, CBO-2 Option 57 p. 65, Pollin 2003, Klien 2020, Schulmeister 2009).

We now have mutual funds, which own stocks and bonds, and exchange-traded funds (ETFs). They will be subject to the transaction tax. We have a menagerie of what are known as derivatives:

> A type of financial contract whose value is dependent on an underlying asset, group of assets, or benchmark... The most common underlying assets for derivatives are stocks, bonds, commodities, currencies, interest rates, and market indexes (Fernando 2024).

Many proposals suggest a transaction tax rate for bonds and derivatives based on their underlying assets. However, it might be best to tax the market value, that is what someone pays for a bond or derivative. (CBO CBO-8, Option 74 p.86, CBO-3 2019 Option 37 p.298, Pollin 2002 p.19-22).

High-frequency trades have increased dramatically since 2006, varying day-to-day and year-to-year — representing up to half the volume today (Seth 2024, Kilen 2020). Much of the high-frequency trade volume will disappear with a transaction tax; that is good because this activity adds little or nothing to the real economy, being a zero-sum poker game.

Of course, reducing the incentive for short-term pure speculation will make the market smaller. Some claim this will increase volatility because the market will have fewer willing buyers (Lysandrou 2013). On the other hand, pure speculation can increase market volatility spectacularly — and is a root cause of many market crashes. A transaction tax reduces the risk of free-falling speculative and computer-driven crashes.

6. The Tax-Free Worker

The need to avoid skewing the market will likely result in different rates for different financial instruments. We should undoubtedly figure it out and adjust if needed. The goal is to create a mix of transaction fees for all financial instruments, even those that may be invented to get around the tax, which keeps the current market balance. The same goes for trying to go off-shore. It is payable by every U.S. resident and citizen.

But why 0.01% or 0.1%? Back in the day, from the 1930s to the 1970s, brokerage fees were much higher than today, and the stock market was just fine. They were about 1% to 2% higher than today (Wile 2014, Aked 2016).

I propose a 0.2% to a maximum of 0.5% transaction tax on stock sales and the sale of all financial instruments at a mix of rates. The rates will be set so that $500 billion is raised annually unless the maximum does not get there, in which case the tax benefits to workers will be lowered. The tax rate can start at 0.02% and go up each month that same amount until the target rate is reached. That will give everyone time to see how the market reacts. Of course, what is not taxed is the company issuing stock or bond in the first place — the actual investment or loan to the company (CBO CBO-8, Option 74 p.86, CBoe -2 2025, Trading Economics 2025).[3]

In addition to a transaction tax for derivatives, the CBO looked at taxing money made on derivatives as ordinary income. They are sometimes used as a "hedge" if an investment goes bad but are often speculative (Ferando-2 2024). On the other hand, at least one case where a food derivative invented by someone at Goldman Sachs may have exacerbated rising prices that began with crop failures in Russia and the United States in 2011 (Bjera 2011, Wiggin 2021). Mortgage derivatives created a mortgage crisis in 2006 (Amadeo 2021). The CBO option has some exceptions:

The option would exempt certain derivatives related to real estate and those used for hedging by businesses. In addition, the option would not extend to employee stock options, insurance contracts, or annuities (CBO-3 2019 Option 38 p.301).

This would yield "only" $3 billion but increase the cost to speculate.

A relatively new financial instrument is crytocurency, Bitcoin being the most well known. Bitcoin is not the only cryptocurrency traded daily. While cryptocurrency started as a good idea, it is now almost entirely pure speculation. Largely unregulated, it is difficult to determine the trading volumes because some traders use bots to create excitement with artificial wash sales in pump-and-dump schemes. Some sources for volume, such as CoinMarketGap, have taken steps to detect artificial trades. Few people buy anything with cryptocurrency, even though some currencies other than Bitcoin have tied for a stable currency, such as tying its value to the dollar.

The proposal is to tax cryptocurrency and cryptocurrency ETF transactions involving a United States resident or citizen who has a stake in the trade in any way. What is exempt from this tax is actually buying a non-financial product or service with cryptocurrency. A conservative estimate is that a 0.5% transaction tax will yield $15 billion. (CoinMarketGap 2024 Statisitic-8 2024, Sharma 2024).

> NEEDED: $296 billion = $814 billion - $500 billion - $3 billion - $15 billion

In 2017, 47 million returns had itemized deductions totaling $1,400 billion. The tax code was changed to raise deductibles that year and is due to sunset in 2025 unless renewed. In 2019, with the higher deductibles in place, the number of returns that had itemized deductibles shrank to 18 million with a total itemized deductions of $645 billion (PNC Insights 2024).

Eliminating itemized deductions is another $102 billion — or, $231 billion when the 2017 Tax Cuts and Jobs Act (TCJA) expires. (CBO-1 Option 14 p.77, see also CBO-8 2024 Option 49 p.59). The best course is to keep the TCJA's higher deductibles and eliminate itemized deductions. This will help simplify the tax code and help low-wage workers.

Eliminating itemized deductions will eliminate a political favorite, deducting mortgage interest. However, coming up with the down payment is the primary barrier to homeownership, so the mortgage deduction does little to promote home ownership (Waters, 2023). Thus, eliminating some or all of the tax burden on wages is a better way to encourage home ownership.

On the other hand, eliminating itemized deductions for mortgage interest and property taxes is may put pressure on housing prices, lowering them — depending on the local market (Harris 2013). As we'll see in an upcoming chapter, the lack of affordable housing is hitting household budgets hard. 80% of the filers using this home interest deduction make over $100,000, so the impact will be on the higher end of the housing market.

NEEDED: 194 billion = $296 billion - $102 billion

Require people who file for the Earned Income Tax credit to have a social security number valid for employment — that is eligible to work in the United States (CBO-8 2024 Option 60 p.71)

NEEDED: $190 billion = $194 billion - $4 billion

Currently, if a high-income taxpayer is actively involved in running a business, as some limited partners and most owners of S corporations are, that person's share of the firm's net profits is not subject to either the additional Social Security tax or the "net investment income tax." (CBO-8 2024 Option 53 p. 63). If taxed like everyone else, it will yield $37 billion a year.

NEEDED: $153 billion = $190 billion - $37 billion

Change how capital gains of a deceased person is taxed. Currently, the inheritors get the asset and don't pay capital gains until they sell it — and the gain is based on what it was worth when they got it. The money made by the deceased is never taxed. This captures the capital gains of the deceased (CBO-8 2024 Option 51 p. 61).

NEEDED $105 billion = $153 billion - $48 billion

Eliminate the last-in-first-out inventory method (CBO-8 2024 Option 66 p. 77).

NEEDED $82 billion = $105 billion - $23 billion

Tax foreign income at the full U.S. rate (CBO-8 2024 Option 65 p. 76).

NEEDED $46 billion = $82 billion - $36 billion

Add 1.5% to the top four tax brackets (CBO-2 2022 Option 13 p.72). Given the tax reduction for the first $14 per hour, anyone making under $275,000 will still get a net tax reduction. Anyone making under $1,000,000 in manufacturing or agriculture will get a net tax reduction.

NEEDED: Zero = $46 billion - $46 billion

This is the American Worker Tax Relief Program. With the trust we discussed, we don't need to depend on accurate revenue assessments from the tax if the money goes into a trust — call it the Worker Trust. It will still work if it doesn't reach taxes on $14/$30; we start at the bottom, reducing the benefit level — $2 per hour for manufacturing and agriculture, to $1 for every other worker. If it goes over, that's fine — adjust the input rates or up the pay levels for which the tax break applies.

6. The Tax-Free Worker

Using the Worker Trust as the intermediary between money coming in and going out means it works even if our estimates of these gigantic numbers are off. The trust will be managed to have a reserve to make sure that the payout is predictable and should be announced every year.

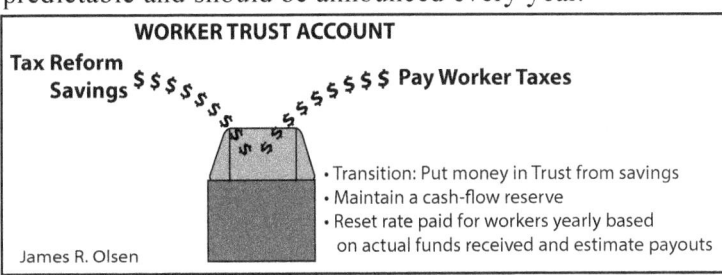

Of course, the Worker Trust may be a bookkeeping device that keeps a balance sheet with income coming in and expenses going out:

PROFIT AND LOSS
  INCOME
  • Increase tax revenue due to changes in the tax code (itemized deductions, earned income limitations, and net investment income).
  • Revenue sources (financial transaction tax, definitives, and added taxes).
  EXPENSES
  • Lost tax revenue due to tax-free portion of pay –> Social Security, treasury.
  • Workman's Compensation offset manufacturing & ag -> paid to states
  • Unemployment offset manufacturing & ag –> employers UI account
  NET INCOME

BALANCE SHEET
  ASSETS
    • Net Accrued Income
    • "Accounts Receivable" - expected income for the rest of the year
  LIABILITIES
    • "Accounts Payable" - expected for the rest of the year
  WORKERS EQUITY
  • Reserve - 25% of next year's est. accounts payable
  • Remaining Equity (Assets - Liabilities - Reserve)

This balance sheet keeps Remaining Equity positive. Then, net income will be accrued in a Workers Trust, which must stay positive to keep this plan tax-neutral. It should be built up with a reserve before implementing the tax relief. Each year, the dollar amount of $14/$30 and/or the transaction tax rates can be adjusted to keep the Workers Trust Net Income Account positive.

The trust serves as a buffer so that the worker benefits can be adjusted to the actual tax reform savings. Even if the estimates have errors or changes happen as the program proceeds, the Workers Trust will always have sufficient "funds." The idea is to avoid the periodic fear that Social Security trusts will run out of money — because Social Security has fixed benefit expenses and variable revenue inputs (Center on Budget and Policy Priorities-3 2024). On the other hand, tax reduction benefits may, if needed, vary year-to-year based on the Workers Trust balance sheet.[4]

There will be plenty of objections, worrying over the effect on financial markets and speculators worrying over being put out of a job. In the end, political will is needed. If we do, we will reduce taxes on the real economy at the expense of pure speculation. It is better than continuing to put band-aids on a gaping wound. This proposal reduces taxes where it counts: the American Worker and their employer.

Lobbyists will come out of the woodwork complaining about their pet deduction and try to get their industry classified for the $30 pool. Hold fast Congress. The focus is on workers whose primary activity is goods manufacturing, farming, ranching, nursery production, fishing, and forestry, as well as their first-level supervisors (BLS-9 2024).

• 7 •
RAISING CHILDREN

Art by Tanya Antusenok

Raising children is an essential activity that costs too much — 24% of household income (Care 2024). As we discussed, the real economy includes the stay-at-home parent raising a child as well as the worker paying for childcare. They should get a break.

There are two things that attempt to accommodate this in the current tax code. One is the Child Credit, which is $2,000 per child with many ifs:

- If wages were earned. Of course, low-income workers may not owe any taxes
- High-income workers are not eligible. (IRS-1 2024).

It turns out that 26% of all children do not get this tax credit, and 90% of them are in poverty. (Collyer 2023).

The second tax code accommodation is the Child and Dependent Care Tax Credit, which pays 20% to 35% of childcare expenses. Again, it would only be helpful for people who pay sufficient income taxes (Parys 2024).

Instead of marginally effective tax credits, we could send each household childcare money. We can help ensure every child is cared for with less financial strain; I propose Child Sustenance Assistance. The amount would be based on the child's age and four income groups.

Different sources have different amounts for average childcare cost and the kind of childcare. Cost varies state-by-state and in metropolitan areas. The base rates used in these calculations are $300 per week for infants and young children 0 to 6 years old and $225.00 a week for older children (Care 2024, Haze 2024, Pine 2023). The Child Sustenance will deliver weekly childcare sustenance to all households with children:
- For children 12 and under:
    - 80% of these weekly averages for people making less than $50,000 a year with all adults working for wages at least 32 hours a week, 65% if an adult works in the home (and can care for a child).
    - 67% for people making $50,000 to $100,000, 52% if an adult works in the home.
    - 50% for $100,000 to $200,000, 35% if an adult works in the home.
    - 7% above $200,000, 5% if an adult works in the home.

  These are feathered to avoid sharp income boundaries.[5]

- For additional children 12 and under in the household:
    - 75% is added for the second child,
    - 25% for the third and fourth child,
    - 15% for each additional child.

7. Raising Children

- For teenagers up to 17 years old:
  - A flat of $35 per week is for people making under $100,000 annually.
  - $900 a year for higher-income families.

This payment would be accompanied by dropping the Child Credit and the child's part of the Child and Dependent Care Tax Credit.

Examples:

Single mother with two children, 4 and 6, working full time for $20,000 per year: provide $420 per week, for $23,300 annually, bringing the total household income to $43,300 per year. From poverty to 165% of poverty.

A single mother with two children, 4 and 6, works part-time 16 hours per week for $7.25 per hour totaling $5,800 per year: provide $367.50 per week for $19,110 annually, bringing the total household income to $24,910 per year, $1,000 below the poverty line.

Two adults, a household income of $75,000, and one 11-year-old child. One unpaid adult works in the home: provide $105.75 per week for $5,499 annually. (The current law would give a child credit for $2,000 for the year.)

Two adults, a household income of $75,000, and one 11-year-old child. Both working: proivide $150.75 per week for $7,839 annually. (The current law for child credit and child and dependent care is $2,600 for the year.)

Single parent, $150,000 per year working full time. $112 per week, for $5,850 per year. (The current law for child credit and child and dependent care would be $2,600 for the year.)

This will cost about $236 billion plus $4 billion to administer this new program (Statista-2 2024, Care 2024, Global Data 2022, BLS-10 2020, Census Bureau-1 2023).[6]

NEEDED $240 billion

Where do we get it? First, look at the complex tax code. This payment duplicates the Child Tax Credit and the Child and Dependent Care Tax Credit for children; these would be repealed. This will yield about $97 billion (York 2020).

> NEEDED $143 billion = $240 billion - $97 billion

Fully legalizing marijuana and tax sales 60%.[7] This will raise $16 billion. Add 19% to the federal alcohol and tobacco tax by 50% yields another $13 billion. (HTS 2024, Office of Trade Representative 2024, CBO-8 2024 Options 69 & 70 pp.80-81).

> NEEDED $114 billion = $143 billion - $16 billion - $9 billion - $4 billion

Instead of having all advertising written off as this year's cost, make half of the amount amortized over five years (CBO-8 2024 Option 67 p.78).

> NEEDED $100 billion = $114 billion - $14 billion

Transportation taxes include airlines, cruise ships, and cars. A tax to support the Federal Aviation Administration includes a 7.5% excise tax on every airline ticket, plus other fees[8] which raised $10 billion in 2023 (Airport and Airway Trust Fund (AATF) 2023). Double these fees to support childcare, adding $25.13 to the average domestic airline ticket.[9]

Over 26 million passengers arrived at a U.S. port in 2023. Tax non-U.S. Flagged cruise ships with over 50 passengers $75 per passenger. Tax U.S. Flagged cruise ships $10 per passenger. Tax $110 for every overnight passenger leaving from a U.S. port on a passenger ship with over 300 passengers; this will yield $4 billion (US DOT 2024).[10]

With over $600 billion in new car sales in the United States, a federal tax of 2.8% would yield $17 billion (Statista-9 2024).

> NEEDED $69 billion = $100 billion - $10 billion - $4 billion - $17 billion

Veterans on VA disability can work and most do.

> The current system of ratings is generally based on physicians' and lawyers' judgments made in 1945 about the effects of service-connected conditions on jobs requiring manual or physical labor. In practice, those effects were estimates of the earnings that veterans were expected to lose in the civilian labor market for a given service-connected disability, on average, and were not linked to the specific labor market experience of the person receiving the rating. Ratings for many medical conditions have not changed since then (CBO-1 2022 Option 10 p.54).

The CBO option is a means test in which any veteran with a household income under $135,000 (not counting the VA benefit) would get full benefits and over that amount they would be incrementally phased out (CBO-8 2024 Option 23 p.21).

NEEDED $32 billion = $69 billion - $37 billion

We could stop here, subtract 15% of the benefits, and still make a difference. However, we can get the rest of the way with a tax at the source of childcare.

The final step can be taken by one of two options.

First, the average tariff rate is 3.3%. The complex tariff laws have some things tariff-free depending on county and product and others having tariffs up to 20% or more. Imports have increased from around $2.6 trillion in 2018 to over $3 trillion in 2022. We have some "special" tariffs on solar panels, aluminum, steel, and imports from China.

Leaving it to Congress, raise tariffs 1% on average. This will raise about $32 to $34 billion (US Customs and Border Protection 2024, HTS 2024).

Second, the CBO has an option for taxing greenhouse gas emissions at the source at $25 per metric ton. Here, I propose a smaller amount to mitigate the impact of energy costs

— $12 per metric ton except for gasoline production. The Congressional Research Service studied the effect of $25 per metric ton and concluded that fuels such as heating oil would increase price by 6%. The impact of $14 per metric ton will be 3% (CBO-8 2024 Option 73 p.84, CRS 2019, Table 2, p.25).

NEEDED Zero = $32 billion - $32 billion.

The way to administer a Child Sustenance stipend is like we did for wages, with the money going into a Childcare Trust, the trust maintaining a reserve, and annually adjusting the weekly childcare payments.

Here are additional thoughts on administering the Child Sustenance Assistance Program. The new program could land in the Social Security Administration of Health and Human Services. It will require a database with a record of every one of the 73 million children in America.

The registration process must be simple — online with telephone assistance if required. The most straightforward way to avoid duplication and discourage fraud is by requiring a Social Security number for the child. The Child Sustenance Assistance Service (CSAS) could assist in getting a Social Security Number for a child who does not have one. Given the complication of some children who are citizens in households with illegal immigrants, some other means may be needed, I suppose. If 20% of the administration budget is allocated to local caseworkers, visiting 1% of the children a year seems possible.

The principle is that sustenance assistance goes with the child. In cases such as divorce, a child in the care of a government agency, or foster care, the presumption is that the money goes to the place the child is living, spent by a person who has legal custody, spent for the benefit of childcare.

7. Raising Children

There will inevitably be some contention, so CSAS must adjudicate when a court is not involved.

In consideration of having the childcare sustenance rate be adjusted according to different costs for different reasons, it will add significant complications, Beyond determining how to survey the regional costs, further administration costs will be incurred when people move or a child has shared custody. It seems best to leave any differential that may be needed to a local government if there economy is booming with high costs and wage

If we implement this childcare initiative, it will have profound effects. It will make the American Worker even more productive by eliminating many lost hours trying to figure out childcare. It will recognize some of the real economic value of a parent in the home.

• 8 •

How Real Estate Causes the Housing Crisis

The most significant investment many people have is their primary residence. In surveys comparing families who own homes versus those who don't, home-owning families fare much better economically. Many factors are involved in this, including differences in where a person stands financially when buying a home in the first place (Zhu 2024, Habitat for Humanity 2024, Yun 2023). But there is a cost, and we are in it now: lack of affordable housing.

A house is a house is a house in the real economy. A 1,500-square-foot house in decent shape is as useful as a 10,000-square-foot mansion. The average house size has doubled since 1970, even though its utility to the family has changed little. From my childhood, a 1,500 or 2,000-square-foot house worked just fine for a family of six.

The average length of homeownership is 8 years (Meyer 2024). If a house stayed the same price, the standard real estate broker fee of 6% would be paid, and title insurance would be bought each time the house turn over. Half the value would be in the pockets of brokers and title insurers the fifteenth time it was sold. Another way to look at it is that each homeowner has to get least 7% more than they paid to avoid losing money on the house.

While we have had recent food inflation, food prices since 1963 have risen slower than overall inflation (Official Data Foundation Food 2024). Housing prices have increased much faster than inflation. In 1963, the median home price was $17,000. Today, it is $412,000. If the 1963 house had only increased at the inflation rate, it would only have cost $170,000 (FRED-1 2024).

But this was a bumpy ride with booms and busts along the way. And this bumpy ride was driven by speculators using the high leverage of real estate loans to flip houses quickly. Of course, as we said, pure speculation is usually zero-sum or negative-sum.

That said, a home with a mortgage is a forced savings plan as the mortgage gets paid down. A primary home, the house the family lives in, is an investment. Since 1973, good quality stocks have appreciated 10% while, on average, real estate has appreciated about half that (Sohns 2024).

However, real estate is easier to leverage. With 20% down and an increase of 5% in the house's value, it yields a 25% return on the cash put down — the down payment. Since real estate has had a boom-and-bust cycle over the years, it has made middle-class millionaires who bought low and sold high while others suffer foreclosure (Drum 2010). It has also made people homeless (Horowitz 2023).

Suppose we remember that savings from wages, the business owner who sunk money into their business, and the stockholder who bought the initial stock offering from a startup are not excess wealth. In that case, a primary residence and some reasonable amount of land for it to occupy are non-excess wealth — up to a point.

A mansion with a bowling alley and an Olympic-sized swimming pool goes beyond what is needed to live comfortably. A vacation house is not a essential for economic activity as a primary residence.

I am not advocating some transfer of wealth. But, if we have to tax wealth — and indeed, the ubiquitous property tax in the United States does just that — we should distinguish between wealth needed for business economics and home economics, the factory and the home people live in, as things essential for providing goods and services — compared to excess wealth such as a second home or 20 acres of manicured landscape around a half-acre homestead.

Pure speculation in the housing market includes "house flipping," where a property is bought and held for a short time in a rising market to make quick money. Sometimes, the flip is a fixer-upper, so the flip includes adding some value to the house, often cosmetically, to improve "curb appeal." About 6% to 8% of the house transfers are house flipping. Of course, most of these are zero-sum in that the original seller would have realized the increasing value if they waited. House flipping can artificially push prices up as the bubble expands until the inevitable bust. (Caporal 2024, Zinn 2024, Lee 2011).

Property taxes fund much of the local government and most schools. However, they can become problematic because they depend on the property's value. "Mills" are applied to determine the tax; a "mill" is 0.1%. Someone in a home for decades will see the valuation of the home rise and their taxes rise, even though the government entities it is funding have no additional burden from this house. Their home provides the same economic function year after year, yet property taxes rise. The country needs to fix this. It is just not fair.

We begin by taxing real estate speculation. First is a transfer tax for a real estate sale. Most states have a low transfer tax or none at all. There are exceptions:

• Delaware has a 4% transfer tax.

- The District of Columbia, Washington, and Hawaii have lower rates but are high enough to have a median tax of over $4,000 (Teiss 2024).

These transfer taxes don't produce much tax revenue compared to property taxes. But, they mitigate house flipping, which usually has little value to the real economy. We could do extract a cost for house flipping by having a much larger transfer tax during the first two years after a sale, such as a 12% tax for the first year (this includes the option-to-buy agreements and other contractual commitments that may be invented to get around the short-term transfer tax time frame). Then, the tax will be reduced by 1% a month during the second year.

To continue our path to make the American Worker more effective, we look for ways to reduce the property taxes on the home. Let us recognize homes serving real economic activity and those that do less. For instance a long term rental serves real economic activity just like home ownership. Whenever a homeowner takes a rental and lists it as a short-term rental on Airbnb or VBRO, they reduce the housing stock for long-term rentals and make more money. The real economic benefit of long-term rentals may now cost more than it should. A higher tax rate on short-term rentals will even the playing field and result in more long-term rentals.

Implement a differential tax rate favoring primary residences and long-term rentals. Further, property tax codes should differentiate the homestead needed to live in versus the mansion. It seems fair for the householder that the first 1,800-square-foot primary residence or long-term rental unit is exempt from property taxes or taxed at a much lower rate. Further, second homes should be taxed at three to five times the rate of primary homes.

The bottom line is that the property tax structure affects the cost of a family's home, whether owned or rented. Property taxes should favor the primary residence and long-term rental, as they are essential to the real economy.

Make Things in America Again

Photo by Gaius, black and white, smudge, texture by James R. Olah

OR

Photo by Fiona_13
black and white texture by James N. Olah

A Fox Guarding Healthcare

Putting insurance companies in charge of healthcare is like letting the fox guard the hen house. Healthcare has grown to 17% of the GDP, costing an average of $22,356 annually for people over 65, $9,154 annually for working-age adults, and $4,217 for children (Andruos 2024, CMS 2023). The United States is an outlier, with the highest per capita costs in the world. But being the highest cost does not make us the healthiest. While we are said to be healthier than 80% of the countries in the world, we don't make the top twenty (Wage 2024, World Population Review, Cox 2024). The American Worker is paying the price for our patchwork system.

There is a way to cut the cost of healthcare burden on the American Worker and the companies that employ them. Study after study ends with the lowest cost and most effective solution — a National Health Plan. The average premiums employers pay for a single worker are over $8,000 a year and over $23,000 for a family (KFF-3 2024). These premiums are $3.40 to $9 per hour for non-small business employers; small businesses are relieved of this burden leaving the employee to find their own health insurance. Employee contributions add another dollar or two per hour (KFF-3 2024). The complicated rules of current law may yield lower premiums for a worker, but they are taxpayer subsidized.

The median healthcare cost is 11% of the household budget for working families; 7% is insurance premiums (Statistic-6

2023). This makes the American Worker unnecessarily expensive and uncompetitive.

The Affordable Care Act (ACA) is complex. It is 198 pages long, making compliance a major chore. The ACA includes a mandate for employers with over 50 full-time employees. It creates a "marketplace" for private and cooperative insurers, requiring coverage for preexisting conditions. The ACA's goal was to get everyone covered, but it fell short of fixing the problem. The uninsured rate is still too high. During its decade-plus history, the uninsured rate went from 16% to 7.2%. Working-age Americans' uninsured rate decreased from 17% to 9.6% (Tolbert 2024, KFF-3 2024). But, 7.2% and 9.6% are not zero.

The ACA got more people insured, but not due to the cost-effectiveness of the ACA. Reducing the number of uninsured people was accomplished mainly by increasing Medicaid enrollees rather than significantly increasing healthcare insurance purchases. The promises made by ACA to reduce healthcare costs have not been fulfilled. Its primary benefit, requiring coverage of people with preexisting conditions, could have been enacted independently (KFF-4 2024, Census Bureau-2 2024).

Sadly, we cannot look to the current American healthcare market for the best way to fix healthcare, as it is not the competitive marketplace that many think it is. It is unique in that what is charged for a visit to the hospital depends on who is being billed! Medicare sets fee-for-service (FFS), while commercial insurers often pay a lot more, often over 100% more (KFF-8 2020, CBO-6 2022).

Private insurers increase rates much faster than inflation. While it might seem that private insurers primarily aim to have lower prices, this is not the case. A primary competitive issue is the breadth of healthcare providers they offer.

Institutions game this game; the result is that Medicare paid 87% of the average health service cost, while private insurers paid 145% — and then built that increased cost into their premiums.

Further, the market is often rigged by big private insurers who make deals with providers to limit discounts that rival insurance companies can provide. This combination of government price setting and marketplace deals by private insurers has not worked to control price increases (CBO-6 2022).

It is time for single-payer healthcare. This proposal responds to most of the objections to bills put before Congress voiced by the Heritage Foundation: It is paid for; it preserves Medicare and Medicaid coverage; it preserves private enterprise; it is designed to avoid additional waiting times — and it costs less money (Paulton 2019).

Contrary to what some would like to believe, the administrative overhead for Medicare and Medicaid is low — 1% to 4%, compared to 17% for private insurers (HHS 2024, CAP20-1 2019, Archer 2011, Heath Care Value Hub 2018). Some note that identifying administrative costs is difficult, so these numbers may be questioned. However, the efficiency of the management of Medicare and Medicaid compared to private insurance will win out because there is little doubt that the administrative burden for healthcare providers is unnecessarily cumbersome because of the multitude of companies and agencies with a multitude of billing rules and requirements for paperwork (Wage 2024, World Population Review, CAP20-1 2019, Brook 2018). The Medicare/Medicaid government infrastructure is the most cost-effective way to manage a single-payer program in the United States.

A single-payer National Health Plan is a "Medicare-for-All plus" program for every American citizen and legal resident. National healthcare will incorporate every medical insurance program, including employer-funded medical insurance.

This has been analyzed by the Congressional Budget Office (CBO) and the RAND Corporation in some detail (Nelson 2022, CBO-4 2020, CBO-6 2022, Burns 2021, Lui-1 2018, Lui-2 2016, Lui-3 2019).[11] This National Health Plan replaces Medicare. Medicare revenues from all sources was $1,024 billion in 2023, with $437 billion coming from general taxes rather than the 2.9% Medicare tax or premiums (Federal Hospital Insurance Board of Trustees 2024, KFF-7 2024).

RAND examined single-payer costs without considering how to pay for them. Nevertheless, they looked at the myriad government health programs and decided whether or not they were to be included in a single-payer program. We'll call these the RAND Studies.

The CBO and RAND cost estimates are similar (CBO-4 2020, Nelson 2022, Lui-3 2019). A CBO working paper by Jaeger Nelson uses the same model and data as the CBO studies but includes ways to pay for it (Nelson 2022, CBO-4). CBO studies go into detail about the five single-payer options. These options are used and modified to construct a National Health Plan.

National Health Plan:
- The program covers all legal residents of the United States and all resident children.
- The program covers medical, vision, and dental with copays similar to those under the ACA.
- The benefits for those eligible for Medicaid will be unchanged, including Long Term Services and Support (LTSS).
- The National Health Plan includes moderate LTSS support beyond Medicaid with assistance rates based on income, up to $50,000 - 80%, $75,000 - 70%, $100,000 - 50%, $200,000 - 25%.

- The program includes medical services (but not disability or lost wages) for workman's comp.
- The program includes outpatient private providers of Veterans Administration (VA) medical services and active and retired military medical services in the Continental United States (CONUS). The VA and DoD medical facilities will stay in place under their own funding.
- It funds emergency services for illegal residents, visitors, and tourists.

There are three tiers.

1. First are those who would be eligible for Medicaid. They will continue to be fully covered for medical care, including LTSS. While the CBO Study has them with no out-of-pocket cost, the proposed plan is to have a copay so that it is "worth something" to use healthcare — a $1.00 copay if they have it and a $10 copay for emergency services if they have it.
2. The next tier is people under 120% of the poverty line. The CBO suggests no copay, but again, some copays remind people it isn't free, a $10 copay and $50 for emergency care — almost a day's work for a minimum wage worker.
3. The third tier is everyone else. The studies indicate that the current copays and cost-sharing average 7.5% of the total cost.[12]

The problem with the CBO studies is that they examine costs projected for 2030 and include a continuous growth in spending on healthcare — from $4,462 billion in 2022 to $6,631 in 2030 — a 47% increase (CMS 2022, Nelson 2022 Table 1 p.43). If we adjust this to the proposed plan and assume the remaining cost growth beyond the rate of inflation does not happen after 2026, we get a similar cost as the one we have here.

With the highest per capita healthcare costs in the world, we want to stop the bleeding and get to a more efficient health system. So, we'll use the CBO information but use values from other sources (CMS 2024).[13]

> HEALTHCARE COST $4,874 billion = $14,500/capita x 334.5 million population

Now, we compute the program size that the taxpayer's healthcare premium will fund. We'll then account for existing taxpayer funded programs and single-payer efficiencies.

The CBO plans include the cost for full benefits for 11 million people not legally in the United States. This plan will fund emergency services for this population. Note that half of them currently have health insurance; private health insurance for those not covered by the National Health Plan will still be available (Passel 2024, KFF-5 2024). The National Health Plan will be for citizens, legal residents, and all resident children and provide emergency services for anyone not in the system, including illegal immigrants and visitors (CBO-4 2020, p. 8).[14]

> SINGLE PAYER COST $4,784 billion = $4,874 billion - $90 billion

The VA and DoD medical services costs outside of hospitals and bases cost $47 billion and $19 billion, respectively. Indian Health Service will stay in place. (VA."Budget." 2023, Defense Health Program 2023).

> SINGLE PAYER COST $4,695 billion = $4,784 billion - $70 billion - 19 billion

Next, we get to savings in administration, replacing the need for providers to bill and manipulate costs for multiple insurers. The estimates in savings vary, but one solid study estimates the savings at $138 billion. In addition, the National Health Plan will eliminate insurance provider excess overhead of $188 billion that finds its way into healthcare costs.

On the other hand, additional enrollees will add $37 billion to the HHS Medicare and Medicaid budgets (CAP-1 2019, CBO-4 2020 pp.78-82, HHS 2024 pp.71 & 81, Health Care Hub 2018).[15]

> SINGLE PAYER COST $4,376 billion = $4,695 billion - $138 billion - $188 billion + 37 billion

We get to the big question. How much more efficient will the American healthcare system be? Efficiency estimates vary widely, with the CBO taking a very conservative approach that efficiency will not improve. The per-capita cost for healthcare in America is $14,500. The next highest countries are $8,000 per capita, Germany and Switzerland. Canada comes in at $6,300, and the United Kingdom (UK) at $5,400 (Wager 2024). While Canada and the UK are known for long waiting times, Germany and Switzerland have some of the shortest waiting times in the world (OECD iLibrary.2024).[16]

Thus, $8,000 per capita is a reasonble target for the United State — of Gemany and Switzerland can do it, why can't we? Even so, $12,340 is used in this calculation —

> The premium rate we calculate is a bit more than Nelson's CBO working paper (Nelson 2022 p.50) though the CBO costs do not seem to assume to include this efficiency. If we cannot get some of the way to Germany and Switzerland, the premium rates below will be 3.5% higher, 1.75% for the employee and 1.75% for the employer — the worker and employer will still pay less than they do now.

$12,340 per capita represents an increase in efficiency for delivering services (in addition to administrative efficiencies) of 15%. However, it is only a 7% improvement over 2019. The United States had a steep rise in health costs during the COVID-19 pandemic — justifiably — and stayed there — unjustifiably (in constant dollars). The disparity discussed earlier between Medicare payments accepted by healthcare providers and those paid to private insurers alone will be more than enough to get us to this price point, about 25% to 35% above current medicare rates (KFF-8 2020). [17]

>SINGLE PAYER COST $3,494 billion = $4,376 billion - $882 billion

The CBO studies estimate the increase in demand of 5% as the system becomes easier to use and increase use of 30% by the 7% uninsured. This is an 8% increase of $213 billion. Further, though our current cost includes LTSS, the CBO predicted a massive increase in its use if it were free. It is not free in our plan, so 25% of the CBO number is used: $100 billion.

>SINGLE PAYER COST $3,807 billion = $3,494 billion **+** $313 billion

This cost must be offset and paid for. So, we estimate the net cost of a national insurance plan. There are offsets, so some federal budget items will no longer be needed with the single-payer system.

>NEEDED $3,807 billion

Medicare payroll taxes of $368 billion will no longer be collected from the America Worker and those that employ them.

Medicare was financed in large part by general taxes of $839 billion in 2024. This federal tax input is growing. We use 72%: $606 billion.[18]

The federal Medicaid cost in 2024 was $541 billion. The Medicaid LTSS and disability program will continue to be funded: $388 billion.

A child health insurance program paid $17 billion (HHS 2024 pp. 71&97&129, KFF-7 2024, KFF-6 2023, Peter G. Peterson Foundation 2024).[19]

9. A Fox Guarding Healthcare

NEEDED $2,796 billion = $3,807 billion - $606 billion - $388 billion - $17 billion

There is a tax exclusion for employer medical plans, which is no longer needed. The additional taxes that will be collected is $391 billion. (CBO-5, Table A-2, p. 19: See also, CBO-1 2022 Option 6 p. 30, Tax Policy Brief Book 2024).

NEEDED $2,405 billion = $2,796 billion - $391 billion

Since this plan replaces ACA, the Premium Tax Credit of $316 billion will no longer apply (KFF-3 2024, Banthin 2013).

NEEDED $2,089 billion = $2,405 billion - $316 billion (If these taxes were to be included in the premium, add 1.3%.)

Take 75% out-of-pocket costs of $442 billion in 2022. (Statista-10 2024).

NEEDED $1,757 billion = $2,089 billion - $442 x 75% billion

The CBO Study proposes paying for this with a "flat tax." However, it is not really a flat tax — taxes that go to the national treasury. Instead, this is a National Healthcare Premium for a group health plan encompassing the entire nation. If we compute a premium as a percent of all income earned, $25.1 trillion, including wages, we get 7.0%.

NEEDED Zero = $1,757 billion - $25,100 billion total income x 7.0% (flat fee)[20]

This is a premium for everyone who has any income. Remember the taxes stripped from workers' pay of 7.5% for the first $14 per hour and $30 per hour if they are in manufacturing or agriculture. This premium is not some tax that goes into the void; this is a healthcare premium for the worker. So, it is only fair that a $14-an-hour worker should pay 49¢ an hour for a great health plan.

By allocating half to the employee and half to the employer, we get:

- 3.5% of income for the wage earner.
  > Net 2.05% = 3.5% - 1.45% medicare tax eliminated.*
- 3.5% for the employer.
  > Net 2.05% = 2.5% - 1.45% medicare tax eliminated.*
- 7.0% for self-employed and retired.
  > Net 4.1% = 7.0% - 2.9% medicare tax eliminated.*
  * Medicare tax goes up another 0.9% after $200,000 in income.

So, right now, you are paying 1.45% of your wage for a medicare tax, which delivers no immediate benefit if you haven't retired. How would you like to pay 2.05% more and get a great health insurance plan now?

Compare this to the current system with tax subsidized rates. The average gold plan for the ACA is $488 per month (KFF-1 2024). With the proposed plan, anyone making less than $167,000 will pay less than that. The average premium is around $700 per month. Anyone making under $240,000 will pay less. Of course, it is progressive — people making more will pay more — $500,000 with a healthcare premium of $1,458 a month and $1 million, $2,916 a month.

Like the Workers Trust, a Healthcare Trust will be set up to receive a revenue stream and used to pay medical bills.

There are no deductions for this. Employers will withhold the tax at a rate of 3.5% and send that and their share to the Healthcare Trust. Any adjustments for non-wage income are reconciled on tax returns. Like the other trusts, it is self-adjusting; the benefits are adjusted annually depending on the trust balance sheet. For the Healthcare Trust, the percentages for the LTSS should be adjusted first for new residents and then for ongoing residents, giving a buffer before raising the premium.

A risk in the CBO single-payer scheme is prices for medical services will be set by the agency when it has essentially become a monopoly. We need a market mechanism. The CBO analysis assumes that a service provider who chooses to sell services outside of Medicare-for-All cannot participate; they get to decide year by year. And private insurance would be prohibited (Nelson 2022, CBO-4).

But if there is no market mechanism, how will prices be determined? I understand the desire to avoid the wealthy capturing the best of the healthcare industry. However, a market mechanism is required to align the price of a service with the actual cost of services with a reasonable profit by private providers subject to a healthy competitive environment.

To retain a competitive environment, this proposal lets private enterprises have it, as long as everyone is paying the National Healthcare Premium. There will be things like optional plastic surgery that a National Health Plan will not pay for. If an outfit has healthcare services that overlap with those provided by the National Health Plan, they will provide that service with the same quality at the same rates for some minimum percent of their business — 25%.[21]

The challenges experienced by other countries with single-payer plans include long wait times due to limited medical capacity (Ross University 2021, Caring Support Blog.2023). The estimate for the cost of the proposed program is higher than estimates that constrain supply and exceed the per capita rate of single-payer countries with short waiting times. It is essential to pay healthcare providers enough to pay their staff well and have enough of them so that long wait times are avoided.

On the other hand, there must be mechanisms so that paying well leads to the desired results rather than excess profits or senior management compensation. To further create a competitive market, the National Health Program can provide financial incentives for performance, patient safety, quality of service, wait times, availability of services, wellness programs, and integration of proven naturopathic practices.

We have now stripped American Workers of much of their tax burden, provided workers in the paid workforce and unpaid work in the home with childcare support, suggested how to get workers an even break for housing, and dealt with healthcare.

Nationwide healthcare will profoundly affect household budgets, worker productivity, and the competitiveness of the companies they work for. We used studies that estimated the GDP impact for three of our initiatives and came up with a slight positive. But, when taken together, the whole is greater than the sum. The productivity of the American worker will trickle up, boosting the monetary economy and the real economy and raising both the monetary GDP and the real domestic product.

Our trickle-up economics will have another effect: to take people who are being supported by the taxpayers, most of whom would work if they could, and put those who are able to work.

· 10 ·
WANTS TO WORK BUT CAN'T

Attempts to eliminate poverty in the United States have been tricky and sticky. The tax reform proposed in this book with move some families out of poverty. Eliminating the social security tax on the working families in poverty will move would have moved the poverty rate needle in 2023 from 11.1% to 10.9%. For families with children the impact is more dramatic, estimated to bring down the poverty rate from 11.1% to 10.1%.[22] But, more work needs to be done.

Politicians often oversimplify the problem because there are many reasons and causes for poverty. The setting can be urban or rural, homeless, a single parent, mentally ill, cognitive disability, physically disabled, addicted to drugs, or the cultural setting in which a person grew up. We can read of famous Congress people who lived through difficult times in Brooklyn, farm country, and the rust belt (Chisholm. *Unbought and Unbossed*; Tester, *Grounded: A Senator's Lessons on Winning Back Rural America*; Vance, *Hillbilly Elegy*).

The remnants of institutionalized racial segregation and prejudice and current prejudice are suggested by the data on the number of people in poverty, with 21% Native American, 18% Black, and 17% Hispanic. The average is 11%. Better than average, with 9% Asian and 8% White only (Statista-5 2024). This is one reason but not the only reason. Poverty is real no matter what the background; mental illness is real no matter what the background; addiction is real no matter what the background.

> I live in Ravalli County, Montana, where the Yellowstone TV series set was located — they filmed on our streets. A few stories as an employer gave me a sense of the maze people getting government assistance to walk through. Each person walking through this maze, trying to find a place to live, food, transportation, access to the Internet, clothes, laundry, and the list goes on — things many of us take for granted — walking the maze involves dealing with multiple government agencies, each with their own rules.
>
> ***
>
> One of my company's projects involved teaming up with a non-profit led by a clinical social worker who had a lot of experience with veterans. We got a grant that helped my open an Internet Café that

10. Wants To Work But Can't

served the general population and high-functioning people with mental illness. We set it up so that customers could use tokens — bought or given to those who could not afford it — to eliminate the stigma of needing assistance. My company hired high-functioning peers part-time.

One of our part-time employees was very intelligent and in charge of IT, but he had little work history because of his mental health issues. He lived in the community, in subsidized housing, receiving mental health treatment, but had no driver's license. We paid him $400 a month.

One day, he says he has to quit because he is making too much money! Someone was telling him he would get kicked out of his apartment. Now, I have a master's degree in engineering, and I couldn't follow the Byzantine set of rules he was trying to navigate. Ultimately, the only thing I could come up with was to increase his benefits and reduce his pay to ensure he wasn't "making too much money."

I was later invited to a room full of providers, including the Montana Department of Health and Human Services. I told this story. They could not agree among themselves what our employee do — and most had master's degrees. Obviously, the rules of the game get in the way of employment.

***

My wife had a going business in art wear. Wanting to retire from production, we trained three people to silk screening and batik her designs. I watched a woman working on a design with her head a few inches above the shirt.

"Do you need glasses?"

She answered, "I can't afford them."

I picked up the phone and called my ophthalmologist. I told them I was sending someone over to get an eye exam and glasses and that they could send me the bill. This is not that unusual — I know a lot of small business owners who would do the same thing, at least in Ravalli County.

Small things can become disasters for people with little money and no credit cards. I have seen it: Needs $35 in cash to make the rent right now; a broken car that stays broken until the money is cobbled together to get it repaired; a sick child that means no paycheck.

Most people struggling with money, mental health issues, or physical challenges that I know with try to figure it out on their own. This is my experience, certainly different than some political rhetoric, "welfare moms and deadbeat dads playing the system."

Of course, there are few that fit the political rhetoric. But, focusing on the few without accounting for the many has created a complex maze and overburdened bureaucracy built by our lawmakers. The result is an often insurmountable barrier for someone forced to understand the system, frequently feels powerless because they depend on it, and have little time to break free.

Legislators across the land and Congress have passed laws to help but have ended up with piecemeal laws that trip over each other. Each carefully sets limits and rules so no one can exploit the system. Each asks a different department to set up a system to manage this slice of relief. On the street, it creates so much overhead and overlaps that it's a miracle anything gets done.

> My company owned an office building, and one of the tenants was the provider who worked with victims of crime. One day, she came to my office and

said a woman she was working with was about to be kicked out of her apartment because she didn't have the rent. Our provider had put in the paperwork for a rent subsidy, but it was probably a couple of months before it got processed. I wrote a check for $200.

Women who suffer domestic abuse get a protection order and leave with their children, only to find she has little money and no job. I decided to provide a small grant, about $2,500 a year, totally unrestricted — the only rule was that our provider decided it was needed. I didn't need any reports or paperwork, but our provider couldn't even use it without running it through the local domestic abuse shelter.

I did get the report I didn't ask for, and it was amazing how much "leverage" that money had. It filled in the gaps of people struggling to get through life: a little gas money, some grocery money, and clothes for the kids. The whole government and grant scheme is just too bureaucratic.

After a year on a waiting list, many people find they cannot use a low-income housing voucher because they cannot find a "fair market rent"; rentals on the market are above that. It seems simple enough to look at market rentals and ensure a rental is not out of bounds. The list was recently closed in Montana, although 40% of those who got vouchers can't use them (Ambarian 2024, HUD 2024).

I suggest each state legislature, and Congress set up a committee that doesn't have hearings but rolls up its sleeves and walks through what someone has to go through in your state with some people who have walked through it — the actual person, the actual direct provider, not just their bosses. Then, simplify it so that the people you are trying to help don't spend half their time trying to figure out the rules of the game — sometimes the best thing to do is write a check with no strings attached. There is evidence that impoverished people can figure out how to budget their money better than the government (Center on Budget and Policy Priorities-1 2023, Center on Budget and Policy Priorities-2 2021, IRS-2 2024, Lexington Law 2024, Thompson 2018, Abba 2023).

Of course, the family, extended family, a teacher, a coach, or somebody that gives a child a boost. That is part of the story for Chisholm, Tester, and Vance; there were some tough times, and some people cared about them and helped them along. Sometimes, it's not there, and sometimes, it's just the opposite: a home of violence and fear — the tough row to hoe. Many survive it, though the scars are almost always there to see if you get to know them. Some are crushed.

It has been tried with partial success. Welfare-to-work programs did get people off welfare, but not always out of poverty. I availability of childcare makes a difference, so the Child Sustenance Assistance Program will make a difference (Gibson 2018, Sanzenbacher 2023, Tanner 2022). But, this alone will not be as good as we can get.

So, let's get some people out of poverty. Each situation is different.

I sat in meetings with mental health peers and their providers; it became clear that the sum of all programs was not enough. There is a severe lack of caseworkers. If we want successful transitions from welfare to work, we need more well-trained, highly motivated case workers to raise someone out of poverty.

While the math show that added income from tax reform gets some people out of poverty, the unmeasurable is that providing help where it counts, wage tax relief, childcare, and healthcare, removing some of the barriers for entering or reentering the workforce, a personal helping hand is bound to improve outcomes. We have relieved the states of some of

10. Wants To Work But Can't

their Medicaid and workman's comp burden. If a state legislature were to take a quarter of that and hire case managers to help some of the 11% of people in poverty get through life, the results will be surprising — and boost the economy. While many are unable, some are unwilling; many will take the lift if offered for real.

We now have tax breaks, health coverage, and childcare help – a boost to lift people up. I suspect this will create a new cadre of people seeking work.

78 Make Things in America Again

Photo by Goredenkeff, exended up, black and white, texture by James R. Olsen

• 11 •
WASTED ENERGY, MISSING JOBS

Now we look at other things affecting the working family's budget. We begin with the tax code and the cost of preparing taxes. There are 12 schedules and 100 forms associated with the individual tax Form 1040. I could not find a complete list of tax credits and deductions that represent "good ideas" that come forth from Congress and end up in the tax code. Some are necessary, but others encourage or discourage specific economic activities, including energy-efficient homes, plug-in vehicles, lifetime learning, American Opportunity Credit, etc. The list goes on long enough that many people do not have the time to figure it out — so Congress was generous enough to allow a person to deduct the cost paid to someone to prepare a return. The complex tax code is a waste of energy.

This burden on the American Worker can be reduced by going through every credit and deduction, removing those from the individual tax code, and moving those with merit to the service or product as a price reduction — a negative Value Added Tax (VAT) if you will.[23] Every example listed above is a candidate for elimination — if Congress thinks they are good public policy, take it out of the individual tax code and credit it to providers.

Next, we turn to the household energy bill, which pure speculative enterprises are driving up. First and foremost is cryptocurrency (crypto) mining. Bitcoin (and other cryptocurrencies) started as an exciting idea of alternative money. However, it quickly became purely speculative, adding no value to the real economy. It is sometimes used for buying and selling; criminals and terrorists find it useful for untraceable transactions. One reason for the growth of crypto mining in the United States is that China was smart enough to ban the practice (Varun 2024, crypo.com 2024).

Crypto mining is a big subtracter with no useful utility for the real economy — mining a single bitcoin uses enough energy to power 61 homes for a year in the United States (NFTEvening 2024). While about half use some sort of renewable energy, including hydro-power, it is unnecessary because it is yet another poker game — crypto-speculators may want to get a "how win at poker" book instead (U.S. Energy Information Administration 2024). Crypto mining energy from the grid should be taxed so that the cost of power is 100 times that of residential users.

Next on the hit parade are Artificial Intelligence (AI) server warehouses. AI can be good, bad, and ugly. Start with energy use. Nearly every hi-tech company and online retailer in America is rushing to AI, which means incorporating software innovations into electronic hardware that consumes electricity. Of course, "cloud server farms" have already sprouted, but AI will take five to ten times the energy per square foot.

The total energy goes up as more computing is packed into every square millimeter on chips. More computing power packed into a microchip means more heat. This is why water cooling is about to take over from air cooling in server farms. The industry is looking for more renewable energy. Even so, this is quickly becoming an energy user that will drive up the household energy bill (Cohen 2024).

11. Wasted Energy, Missing Jobs

AI does contribute to the real economy. It is the latest technology to increase worker productivity. Even so, power rates should favor households, businesses, farms, and factories. One way to look at the business use of electricity is payroll per megawatt hour; the higher the number, the better. A wood shop scores very, very, very high compared to AI server warehouse.

Suppose we set the power rate higher for AI and cloud servers by taxing or setting rates 25% to 100% higher than for other users. The industry will be more motivated to look for energy and chip-cooling efficiency.[24]

Artificial Intelligence promises to make many software-driven processes more efficient, including targeted advertising. It is also the latest automation that threatens to replace humans in two ways.

One is the accelerating the replacement of online customer service, which many online retailers already automate. Many believe AI will improve the accuracy and quality of automated customer service and optimize the cost of delivering online retail orders. There has already been a move to use AI to replace some software programmers. It promises to improve automated driving. The list goes on in nearly every industry. I do not believe in overly worrying about replacing human jobs: tools to reduce human effort are as old as the lever.

Two is more concerning — human creativity. Generative AI replaces human creative products, from novels to artwork. *AI is not creating original work.* Rather, it provides a response that is a synergy of a body of human creativity. Sometimes, it plagiarizes.

There are several lawsuits because, it can be massive plagiarism. Some AI companies have started licensing human creative works for their learning algorithms — as it should be. (Levin - Author's Guild 2024)

Further, the buyer of a piece of art or novel often does not know if it is partly or wholly AI-generated. Some publishers try rectifying this, but they usually take different approaches.

Congress needs to fix this — the creative American Worker needs protection. First, all AI generative companies should:
1. be required to include in any generated piece that it is AI generated, give it a unique serial number and a watermark, and store a copy,
2. be required to record which human or business generated it.
3. require the purchaser to leave the AI notice intact.
4. require that training systems license any copyrighted material for training.
5. require all artwork, books, and other media to disclose if AI was used.

Further, the generator of IA-generated works is not presumptively protected by copyright — it will be incumbent on the generator to show that the source material for training was public domain or licensed and that the input and parameters are themselves original art that produced a unique piece that has unique artistic nontrivial merit. The input and parameters are what is the original copyright, the generated output being derivative of the entire body of material used to train the AI system.

Congress should explicitly state that software is not human and does not enjoy a First Amendment right. Further, the daily slander generated by bad actors is too hard to keep up with in any practical way. Thus, closing all loopholes is warranted:
1. Any use of AI or other software manipulation to know-

ingly create a falsehood about any private person shall be a misdemeanor and subject to slander and liable.

2. Any use of AI or other software manipulation to knowingly falsely create a pornographic image or act of any person shall be a felony as well as subject to slander and liable.

3. Every social media provider, upload service, sharing service, or other publisher shall be required to register the actual name of any user and shall take steps to prohibit the posting of such material and remove it immediately upon notice. This applies to all services, regardless of location, that provide service to URLs in the United States. VPN-like services provided within the United States shall, upon notice, block access to any provider found to have violated these provisions.

Let us bring some jobs back to America. It is cheaper and more accessible for someone sitting in a call center in India to get a United States phone number than to sign up for T-Mobile or a so-called burner: Tracfone, mintmobile, tello (iTeleCenter 2024). Phone numbers are managed by the Federal Communications Commission (FCC), which has delegated the job to a company called Neustar to assign phone numbers (Plum|voice 2024). Furthermore, Neustar hands out phone numbers to Voice over the Internet Protocol (VoIP), telephone companies, and cell phone networks.

The FCC scheme led to call centers for customer service moving from the United States to places with cheaper labor, such as India. Then, this cheap overseas service led to another kind of call center — the scammer and spammer, which extracted $56 billion from Americans in 2023 (LaMont 2024).

Congress and the FCC should put a stop to it. Require any United States phone number to be allocated only to a legal resident of the United States or business registered in the United States with a physical location in the United States located in the area served by the area code.[25] If anonymity is essential, assign a unique code for prepaid phones sold in America.

If it is essential to have VoIP codes assigned for overseas use, identify a specific unused area code —area code 200 seems to be unused — so everyone knows the call does not originate in the United States. Even so, it requires a verifiable account holder. This is where a tariff might make sense as we seek to add Americans to the workforce.

Most jobs do not last forever, so people will find themselves unemployed. It is the employer that pays unemployment insurance (UI). Federal law sets a framework for UI, which each state manages. State laws differ, though most states provide payments to people who have been employed for a year and have been involuntarily laid off. The benefit usually lasts up to 26 weeks. During most recessions, including the one caused by the COVID-19 pandemic, Congress and state legislatures extend benefits. Of course, individual circumstances get lost in all of this, leading to family disasters — sometimes going from a good job to homelessness.

It needs to be reformed. UI reforms have been considered, including in Stephen Wandner's book *Transforming Unemployment Insurance for the Twenty-First Century: A Comprehensive Guide to Reform* (Wandner 2023). While Wandner is hesitant to recommend them, he notes that a National UI system would be the most efficient and consistent way to manage unemployment insurance (Wandner 2023, pp. 109-110, Appendix A, pp. 235-241).

If you are unemployed because of sickness or an accident and cannot work, you are not eligible for unemployment in most states. New Jersey fills this gap with a Temporary Disability Insurance system for which the employer pays 0.1%

to 0.7% and employees less than 0.2% of wages. 25% of the claims were complications of childbirth. It pays 85% of wages for low-wage workers and requires medical certification. Of course, it is not paid if it overlaps with workman's compensation disability. Benefits payments are limited to 70% of average wages in the state for 26 weeks.

Even so, there is a gap because Social Security disability is only available after a year or more, 52 weeks. Even in New Jersey, this gap should be filled with a disability system for 52 weeks — the cost should not double, as the average time in New Jersey on temporary disability was 68 days in 2019. A 25% to 35% increase is a fair bet (New Jersey Dept. of Labor 2020).

Filling these gaps will help the American Worker.

During the COVID-19 shutdowns, several people called for a new version of the Depression-era WPA (Works Progress Administration). One of my uncles worked for the WPA during the Great Depression; it was certainly more productive than standing in a bread line (Wikipedia "Great Depression in the United States"). Some thought of infrastructure and at least one idea of what was in significant shortage during the pandemic in the United States: contract tracers. (Malone 2020). During a time of massive unemployment, like the Great Depression or Great Recession (Wikipedia "Great Recession"), rather than handing money to do nothing, the WPA did public works projects. WPA jobs could be anything from trail work to office work to professional assistance to a government agency.

The idea of UI benefits is to give workers a chance to find another job. The timeline for benefits might look like this:

a. 14 weeks, search for a suitable job.

b. For the next 12 weeks (or during any extended benefits period), accept any job you can perform that pays at least 75% of your previous wage. If offered, accept work for a

WPA position for 24 hours a week or fewer hours. This gets to the standard 26-week benefit term in most states.

c. 8 weeks, benefits extended if working on a WPA program.

A WPA program can be proposed and approved by the American Unemployment and Temporary Disability Insurance Administration by any government agency. Approval is based on suitability, competition with ongoing private enterprises, and a supervisory certification for compliance with non-discrimination, background checks, and basic supervisory skills. The labor will be free to the WPA program since UI benefits are paying for it

Does illegal immigration take American jobs? I don't know. I do know that people in desperate circumstances do desperate things, and we need to be mindful of that. I don't have a good answer.

> My grandfather was in Shanghai in the 1930s working for RCA, when he met a Russian woman. He was divorced. They ended up getting married and she came to the United States.
>
> The Russian woman he met was a refugee. She was from a middle-class family in the port city of Vladivostok when the Red Army was approaching the last act of the Russian Civil War. Her parents were on the wrong side.
>
> Her parents and their friends bought train tickets for their school class and sent them to Shanghai — she never saw them again. The trip did not go as planned, but they made it. She was twelve. When her class got to Shanghai, they had little money and were no longer citizens of Russia because Lenin declared that anyone leaving was no longer a citizen — they were stateless and stuck.

11. Wasted Energy, Missing Jobs

Desperate people do desperate things.

There are 11 million undocumented workers in the United States, about 4.8% of the workforce (Passel 2024, New American Economy 2024). Do they take American jobs? Right now, in January 2025, this is *higher* than the unemployment rate and half of those a what is called "frictional" — people transitioning from one job to another. The math suggests that many or even the majority of these workers are doing jobs for which no citizen is available. The smart thing to do is to find out who is contributing to the economy doing work that no citizen is available to do and give them a work permit. There are two ways to find out.

First is to tighten reporting and compliance. Currently, every employer must fill out a form (Form I-9) authenticating the right to work for each new hire. The employer may not demand specific documents. In particular, a Social Security Card can be presented but is not required. Take a year and require every employee and contract worker to get a Social Security card (which requires a birth certificate) if they don't have one or are a non-citizen with an authorized work permit or permanent resident (these are all picture IDs).

Create a consistent enforcement mechanism. Require an IRS form, containing a list of Form I-9s. Require a statement as to whether or not the list includes all employees. Require any business to pay a tax of $10 an hour or half their pay, which ever is more, for each worker they don't document — over $200,000 a year in extra taxes.

To eliminate a common work-around, require any business with over 50 employees to prepare a Form I-9 for each independent contractor who provides more than 500 hours of direct labor for a business — even if they are provided by a vendor. This will create an incentive to report accurately or face the possibility of tax fraud.

Second is just a thought since I haven't gone through the implications. After giving time for this to take hold, the employer will not be required to fire an undocumented worker. Instead, there will be a moratorium on any penalties if they identify the worker and advertise the job, including on the UI job site — of course for at least minimum wage. Suppose there are no qualified takers in three months. In that case, the undocumented employee is issued a work permit and immediate family residence permit unless they fail a criminal background check — the economy is obviously using their labor. They are not taking a job an American citizen wants.

Illegal drugs affect American Workers.

Once, I was asked to be on a conference call that included two people who grew up in Jamaica. The Jamaican military wanted an airborne remote sensor to track ships and boats.

I asked, "Why in the world does the Jamaican military need this?"

Silly question — drugs. They said, "Look at a map. Jamaica is in the middle of a triangle, the guns come for Haiti; the drugs come from the Yucatan Peninsula, and the customers are in the United States."

Well, it was a hard problem. Finding a cigar boat scooting through a bunch of yachts or a small plane dropping from the clouds 24/7 required more than a couple of sensor aircraft. By the time we got done conceiving a system that would work, a sensor net, tie in with air traffic control and U.S. sensors, the data correlated and synthesized in an operations center, we were past what they could afford — and the drug lords have more money than the country of Jamaica — so even if we built it, they would find a way around it. Drugs come through every which way, in shipping containers, for instance — think about how many containers arrive daily.

The burning question is one we never really answer. Why are the customers in America? If we answer that, we will save lives and make the American Worker more productive by eliminating this tragic burden from families nationwide.

Mental health and addiction are tragic personal problems — and an economic drag. Investing in mental health and addiction is part and parcel of improving the well-being of the American Workforce and making America more productive. What happens now is that there is separate funding and often disjoint treatments for mental health and addiction, even though a high percentage of mental illness is accompanied by addiction — often self-medication. Integrated care works better.

The second thing that happens to people who make progress is that they need help getting into the workforce. As I said, work is often great therapy, but the support systems and funding will still need to be there. This needs to be added to Medicare-for-All. If we do it, I suspect it will pay for itself (Mental Health America 2022, SAMSHA.2021).

Photo by Wasan Tita, crop, black and white, texture James R. Olsen

• 12 •

THE AMERICAN WORKER
TICKLE-UP ECONOMICS

Trickle-down economics, or supply-side economics, was popularized during the Reagan Administration and became the theory for most Republican administrations ever since. As an economic theory, it is a response to Keynesian economics that drove much of Franklin Delano Roosevelt's New Deal in the 1930s as the country and the world tried to recover from the Great Depression. The basic idea of supply-side is that lowering taxes, particularly for the wealthy, stimulates the economy, producing more tax revenue that then is used to reduce the deficit. This has become an excuse not to balance the national budget.

While the need to balance the budget is often stated as an urgent need, the two Presidents who delivered on it in recent times were Lyndon B. Johnson and Bill Clinton.

Pre-pandemic, the Trump administration continued the Republican economic playbook. Surprisingly, the Biden administration announced "modern supply-side economics," even after the record-setting deficits created by handing out a second round of money in 2021 during the COVID-19 pandemic; this combination of tax funded handouts and stimulus spending fanned inflation for the next three years (Lawder 2022, Timiraos 2024). The 2020 COVID-19 stimulus provided massive cash injection during shutdowns that had done its job, but another one was unnecessary.

Biden's economic plan has little resemblance to Reagan's supply-side. Instead of a tax cut, it simply injected government money into the economy. The administration aspired to increase infrastructure funding while making the American Worker more productive — the administration did the former but failed in the latter. President Biden's plan included government-funded worker training and funding things like the National Semiconductor Training Center. Worker productivity initiatives were limited to training — half measures at best (Omeokwe 2022, Biden 2024, Reiff 2024).

We have a $1.9 trillion deficit that the U.S. taxpayer has to pay interest on. Tickle-down, supply-side economic tax policies have been implemented and tried for decades. The bottom line is that supply-side, trickle-down economics did not work to reduce deficits (Rasool 2024, Rainey 2018, Evens 2024, Harper 2023. Gwartney 2024, Liberto 2024). The Democratic counter of infrastructure funding and worker training has not worked either.

It's time to try trickle-up by making the backbone of the economy more productive, the American Worker — who has been shackled to a ball and chain for tax burdens and rising childcare expenses: unfair housing practices and one of the most inefficient healthcare systems in the world.

Decreasing the tax burden on the American Worker and decreasing the largest items in the household budget, childcare, healthcare, and housing, will:

- Increase household savings,
- Increase investment in business,
- Increase consumer spending,
- Make American businesses more cost-competitive, especially manufacturing and agriculture.

We did this by:

- Eliminating federal taxes on wage earners and their employers for the first $14 and the first $30 in pay for manufacturing and agriculture. In addition, we provided relief to manufacturing and agriculture employers for state-collected fees for workman's comp and unemployment insurance.

> We "pay" for it with a net-zero change to the tax code, starting with a tax focusing on speculation, a 0.2% to 0.5% tax on stock and other financial transactions. We add an increase in tax on the four highest tax brackets of 1.5%, though most of them will still come out ahead because we eliminated their taxes with the $14/$30 tax break. We simplified the tax code by eliminating itemized deductions and other tax reforms.

• Providing childcare for every child in America, including those raised by a parent in the home, as we recognize that the real domestic product includes household activities.

> We pay for this with several tax reforms and increased taxes on airline tickets, cruise ship port calls, and new car sales. We increase tariffs an average of 1.0%, leaving to Congress what to tax.

• Creating differential property tax rates that favor primary and long-term rentals over second homes, mansions, and short-term rentals. Add a transfer tax for the first year to inhibit speculation and house flipping.

• Significantly reducing healthcare costs. We select the best approach from the literature and budget studies, which turns out to be Medicare-for-All. We abandon inefficient insurance schemes, including Obama Care and the need for private medical insurance. We include support for long-term assisted care.

> We pay for it with a flat fee of 3.5% of net income while eliminating the medicare tax for a net of 2.05% for the worker and the business that hires them.

- Reforming Unemployment Insurance by implementing the most cost-effective way to manage it. A National Program relieves the states of the program, except for adjudicating claims, because the rules vary from state to state. We implement the best-of-breed, which is found in New Jersey. We include short-term disability insurance implemented in New Jersey and some other states.
- Implementing policies to keep energy bills from rising for the American Worker due to the massive energy demands for cryptocurrency and the lost jobs and scams created by how telephone numbers are handed out. We suggest a fair plan, a bold plan, to make jobs held by illegal immigrants available to the American workforce — and give a work permit to those not in demand by the American workforce.

The sum of all of this is the American Worker ends up with a lot more money in their pocket, making it easier to go from poverty and welfare into the workforce.

A foundational principle of America is that the economy's very purpose is to serve the needs and aspirations of the American workforce. One needs to read no further than "Life, Liberty, and Pursuit of Happiness," a phrase that applies to every American, not just the powerful and wealthy. Of course, the American ideal is that happiness isn't handed out; one should work for it.

The American economy is built on its householders and workforce. We make a more productive workforce by making capitalism work better for the worker. A more productive workforce will trickle-up to create a stronger and more competitive American economy.

END

ENDNOTES

1 Some question the authority to impose income taxes or the actions of the Federal Reserve; this his how it is implemented and enforced. Congress can change it.

Tracing the authority of income tax and Federal Reserve:

U.S. Constitution and Congressional Authority for printing money, operation of the Federal Reserve, and Collect Income Tax

US CONSITITUTION

We the People

National Archives

We the People of the United States, in Order to form a more perfect Union, establish Justice, insure domestic Tranquility, ... do ordain and establish this
Constitution for the United States of America. (https://uscode.house.gov/static/constitution.pdf)

ARTICLE 1, Section 8.
The **Congress shall have Power .. To lay and collect Taxes**... shall be uniform throughtout the United States.

ARTICLE 1 Section 9, **Clause 4.** No Capitation, or other direct, Tax shall be laid,
unless in Proportion to the Census or enumeration herein before directed to be taken.

Section 8, Clause 5: **To coin Money, regulate the Value** thereof.

Congress legislated this to Dept. of Treasury

31 U.S. Code § 5114 - Engraving and printing currency...
Fed order $ \ Delivers $

FEDERAL RESERVE ACT
Chapter 6 of the 62nd **Congress;**
Approved Dec. 23rd, 1913; 38 tat. 251

said Federal reserve bank shall become
a body corporate... shall have power—

Eighth. Upon deposit with the Treasurer of the United States
of any bonds... to receive from the Secretary... circulating notes ... .
.. such notes shall not be limited to the capital stock of such... bank.

Sec A2. The Board of Governors ... shall maintain long run growth of the
monetary ... the economy's long run potential to increase production, so as
to promote the goals of **maximum employment, stable prices, and moderate
long-term interest rates**
https://www.govinfo.gov/content/pkg/COMPS-270/pdf/COMPS-270.pdf

*Generally - the Act allows setting up Federal Reserve Banks as corporations
with Capital Stock to which other banks may subscribe. While the Treasury
prints money, they do so in response to a bond from the Federal Reserve. The
money is given to Federal Reserve Banks who put it into circulation.*

*However, most money in circulation is not in cash, but is numbers on
balance sheets or accounts of banks, businesses, and people. Example
a paycheck. The business writes a check, The check is deposited in the wage
earners account. The wage earner spends it with a debit cards The debit
card amout is added to the businesses account — **no cash changed hands.***

*The primary way the Federal Banks creates money is covering loans from
member banks. Borrow $1 million. The local bank comes up with $100,000. The
Federal Reserve covers $900,000. **$900,000 into circulation out of thin air.***
https://www.govinfo.gov/content/pkg/COMPS-270/pdf/COMPS-270.pdf

Congress legislated controlling the Value a Federal Charter for Corporations, Federal Reserve Banks

Ignores Clause 4

The Revenue Act of 1861
Income tax to finance the Civil War
https://fraser.stlouisfed.org/title/revenue-act-1861-1117

Supreme Court imposes Clause 4
Pollock v. Farmers' Loan & Trust Co
Supreme Court did not say income
tax was unconstitutional but had to be
in apportionment to state population
https://supreme.justia.com/cases/federal/us/157/429/.

Strikes "propotion" clause from constitution

16th Amendment proposed, ratified,
and adopted by Congress.
Article I, section 9, of the Constitution was
modified by amendment 16.

The Congress shall have power to lay and collect
taxes on incomes, from whatever source derived,
without apportionment among the several States,
and without regard to any census or enumeration.
https://www.archives.gov/milestone-documents/16th-amendment

Note: See Newspapers.com or other
newspaper archives for widespread
news on ratificatiom of 16th amemdment

**Congress legislates
Direct income tax without
apportionment**

U.S. Code: Title 26 Subtitle A-Income Taxes
The code begins "There is hereby imposed
on the taxable income of..."

This 2000 page law gives the authority to
the Treasury Dept. who in turn created
the Intternal Revenue Service (IRS)
https://www.law.cornell.edu/uscode/text/26/subtitle-A

James R. Olsen. Includes public clip from
National Archives

2 This is an estimate that has a number of approximations and potential sources of error. The total hours worked is 260 billion (FRED-2 2023), 33 billion of those worked in manufacturing and agriculture (BSL-1 2023). Calculation:

Separate total hours worked into manufacturing/agriculture (ManAg) and all other work. For MagAg, $30 is used. The tax burden and fee burden for both the employee and employer is:

$30 x 15.3% (Social Security/Medicare) = $4.59

    + $2.13 Federal Tax Estimate for Worker (FedTax)

    + $1.09 (Average Workman's Comp for Manufacturing)

    + 30¢ (Unemployment fee support)

= $8.11 per hour.

$8.11 per hour is for someone who is paid at least $30 per hour. Since it is an average some assumptions are made. First the $30 applies to 60% of the manufacturing/ag workforce and $25 for the other 40% who receive $25 or less.

We do the same calculation for the 18% of this population being agricultural workers $25 per hour and $15 per hour: $6.54 per hour.

Combining these —

Total Tax for Manufacturing and Ag = $7.17 per hour x 33 billion hours worked in a year

= $237 billion.

FedTax is computed using the ARRP (ARRP 2024) calculator and the average work week of 36.4 hours for four categories and assign them a weight, and parameters for the calculator:

Single (Si), weight 44%, Single one deduction

Single with one or more children (Sc), weight 1%, Single two deductions

Married no dependents (Mi), weight 27%, Married Joint Filer 2 deductions

Married with dependents (Mc), weight 29%, Married Joint Filer 3 or more deductions

Head Of Household with child was included in the Married

with 3 deductions.

Head Of Household without child was included with Single 1 deduction.

Married filing separately was only 1.5% of the returns and was included with Married

For Married Couples the household income is double the $30/hr wage, then 25% of the wage is subtracted for one spouse as an estimate of the effect of different incomes. Then half that tax is assigned to the worker.

FedTax = Si x 44% + Sc x 1% + Mi x 27% + Mc x 29%

For the remaining paid hours work of 227 billion, the same computations were made for $14 per hour, except they do not include any allocation for Workman's Comp or Unemployment. The result is:

Total Cost of other work = $2.54 per hour x 227 billion hours worked

= $622 billion

The sum for both manufacturing/ag at $30/hr and all other at $14/hour

= $237 billion + $622 billion = $814 billion

3 Some rough comparisons of the transfer tax range given.

The CBO option is for all financial transactions such as stock, bonds, options, futures tax at 0.01% of the contracted value of the transaction. The adjustments for this option were discussed in bit more detail in 2019 (CBO-3 2019 Option 37 p. 298) noting a reduction a short-term trades without stating the amount with a proposed tax of 0.1% and showed $106 billion for 2026. I assume this is still the assumption when 0.01% is used in the current one being used (CBO-8 2024 Option 74 p.86). A rough assumption that the stock market shrink to 80% its current size, then $106 billion from the 2019 CBO option would scale to about 0.38% to raise $500 billion.

The chart for the 2024 CBO option, notes that the 0.01% tax will reduce the value of assets as soon as the option is legislated, showing a $10 billion impact on tax revenue the year before implementation (2025). It shows $10.3 billion for in 2026. A similar number is calculated when scaling the 2024 CBO option.

The CBO amount for jumps to $25.0 billion in 2027. If we assume a 2/3rd loss in half this revenue and scale it to raise 80% of $500 billion we get a tax rate of 0.24%.

If we use the 2024 stock value traded from the Cboe (Cboe 2025) and eliminate 2/3rd of an estimate of the short-term trading a 0.49% to raise $500 million just on stocks and 0.40% is we assume stock transactions are 80% of what will be taxed.

Given my uncertainty of the relative size of financial markets being taxes, 0.5% is a good upper limit of the transaction tax rate for stocks and 0.2% is a good lower limit.

4 Presumably the final authority for setting annual transaction and worker tax relief levels will be the Secretary of Treasury, along with a mandate to set them so as to provide the $500 billion for the Workers Trust — on the advice of a Board of Trustees for the Worker Trust. Since the Securities and Exchange Commission (SEC) oversees the financial markets and the Federal Research has a legislative mandate to manage, in part, for full employment — the trustees of the Workers Trust should include members of both when they advise the Secretary of Treasury as to what rates to set.

Congress should add a mandate the SEC propose a plan to maintain a balanced financial market and recommend transaction tax rates for various financial instruments to the Secretary of Treasury.

5 Feathering around income bracket boundaries is 1% for every $1,000 so that, for instance, instead of 50% at $100,000, it is 49% at $101,000... at $143,000 is 7%. On the other side, $99,000 is 51%... $77,000 is 67%.

6 Estimates for childcare vary. Care.com shows $321.00 per week for infants 0 to 6 years old and $293.00 a week for older children (Care 2024). Trusted Care shows infant daycare $120 to $350 a week and toddler preschool $125 to $250 and in-home family center $125 to $225 (Hazen 2024).

The "Adult Working in the Home" is someone who is not disabled to the extent they cannot provide all of the care needed for children or an adult declared as a non-spouse dependent being cared for in the home.

Calculation: Cost (C_{index}: C_{infant} = $300 per week, by C_{child} = $225 per week) is the cost of care per week adjusted 10% at-home worker — 30% of the households. The population (P_{age}):

$P_{Infants}$ = 22.5 million,
$P_{Years\ 6\ to\ 12}$ = 24.2 million,
P_{Teens} = 25.8 million.

Factors of 25%, 29%, 13%, and 33% are applied to the income brackets ($I_{bracket\ 1\ to\ 4}$) in the plan. This is then adjusted for number of children in household ($N_{children\ 1\ to\ 5}$): 20% one, 41% two, 22% three, 10% four and five, 7% more than five.

For households with more than one child, the supplement is reduced ($M_{child\ 1-5}$): 1 child 100%; 2: 85%, 3 and 4: 60%; 5: 35%. For a house with an infant, it is assumed the the 3rd + children are not infants.

Add $55 per child per year to administer the program to get $4 billion. Thus, the math is:

$COST_{infant} = C_{infant} \times (80\% \times I_{bracket1} + 67\% \times I_{bracket2} + 50\% \times I_{bracket3} + 7\% \times I_{bracket4})$

$COST_{child} = C_{child} \times (80\% \times I_{bracket1} + 67\% \times I_{bracket2} + 50\% \times I_{bracket3} + 7\% \times I_{bracket4})$

$COSTAllAdultsWorking_{infant}$
$= \sum_{children\ 1\ to\ 2} (COST1_{infant} \times N_{children\ 1\ to\ 2} \times M_{children\ 1\ to\ 5})$
$+ \sum_{children\ 3\ to\ 5} (COST1_{infant} \times N_{children\ 3\ to\ 5} \times M_{children\ 3\ to\ 5})$

$COSTAllAdultsWorking_{child} = \sum_{children\ 1\ to\ 5} (COST1_{child} \times N_{children\ 1\ to\ 5} \times M_{children\ 1\ to\ 5})$

$COSTOneAdultHome_{infant} = \sum_{children\ 1\ to\ 2} (90\% \times COST1_{infant} \times N_{children\ 1\ to\ 2})$
$\times M_{children\ 1\ to\ 2} + \sum_{children\ 3\ to\ 5} (90\% \times COST1_{infant} \times N_{children\ 3\ to\ 5} \times M_{children\ 3\ to\ 5})$

$COSTAllAdultsWorking_{child} = 90\% \times COST1_{child}$
$\times \sum_{children\ 1\ to\ 5} N_{children\ 1\ to\ 5} \times M_{children\ 1\ to\ 5}$

$COST_{infant} = 70\% \times COSTAllAdultsWorking_{infant} + 30\% \times COSTOneAdultHome_{infant}$

$COST_{child} = 70\% \times COSTAllAdultsWorking_{child} + 30\% \times COSTOneAdultHome_{child}$

Total Cost = ($COST_{infant} \times P_{infant} + COST_{child} \times P_{child}$ + $35 x P_{teen} x 20% x $35 x 52 weeks + $900 x P_{teen} x 80%) + $4 billion

7 The Federal Government still declares that cannabis is a controlled substance in the United States, even though several states have legalized it for both medicine and rec-

reation. It is long overdue for the Federal Government legalize it (Rozo 2025).

8 $4.80 for every flight segment, $10.60 per passenger to Alaska and Hawaii, $21.10 per passenger for international terminal use

9 Average airline ticket cost from an urban area is $271 (FRED-6 2024)

10 All except one ocean going cruise ship lines are registered somewhere other then the United States, even though they may operate out of a U.S. port (Wikipedia "List of U.S. flagged cruise ships").

11 The RAND Study is based on continuing programs such as Veterans and Indian Affairs. The study assumes workman's comp funds are still collected but reimburse the single pay program for services it provides.

The healthcare cost goes up because unserved uninsured will now seek more healthcare to the tune of another 25%.

Single-payer will eliminate many inefficiens in the system driven by current law, including differential pricing based on who is paying and savings in deferred treatment until it is an emergency, which results in higher use of ambulances and emergency rooms (Committee on the Consequences of Uninsurance. Hidden Cost, Values Lost, Uninsurance in America.)

The RAND study summary (Lui-3, Table 4) shows the total National Spending which includes the government, private insurance, and out of pocket.

12 The plan is more like the Canadian system, which have a single-payer and private enterprise providers as opposed to the UK system where health providers work for the government.

13 By comparison, total healthcare costs used in RAND is $3,823 billion in 2019 (Lui-3 2019), adjusted for inflation to $4,664 billion versus the $4,874 billion used in the calculations.

14 The calculation uses the U.S. average healthcare cost for half of the undocumented population and $2,000 annually for the other half.

15 Medicare and Medicaid manage 39% of the United States healthcare expenditures. According the FY 2025 budget, Medicare has an administrative overhead of 1.1% of funds expended and Medicaid, which is administered by the states, had a 3% overhead on average. The calculation holds Medicaid constant and multiplies the Medicare admin budget by the proportionate growth of 4 times. Then add 10%.

16 While the United States healthcare is 17% of GDP, it is 12% for Germany and for Switzerland. Germany and Switzerland require health insurance under a uniform plan, which is provided by non-profits, the employer being required to participate in Germany. Both allow supplementary private health insurance and Germany allows private insurance instead of the national plan.

Notable differences from the U.S. are standard rates and a national centralize medical records system. Germany and Swiss health plans include long term care and support (Wikipedia "Health Care in Germany," Wikipedia "Health Care in Switzerland," Commonwealth Fund-1 2025, Commonwealth Fund-2 2025)

17 RAND and CBO studies account for administrative savings, but neither appears to account for differential pricing by service providers, which is so large that it creates an uncompetitive environment in the marketplace (KFF-8 2020).

18 If this general fund is eliminated, add 2.41% to the total premiums and require an health provider efficiency improvement of 28% to a per capita cost of $10,470. This is achievable given that this would still be a world record compared to about $8,000 for Germany and Switzerland.

19 Medicare costs used the HHS Budget (HHS 2024):

> Medicare $843 billion = Net Outlays $846 billion - Admin $11 billion - 50% of Related Benefits $10 billion + sequestration $18 billion (p. 71).
>
> Medicaid $151 billion = 28% (percent of Medicaid not LTSS) x $540.89 billion (p. 89).

20 These estimates for revenue raised by the 7.0% fee uses for total personal income in the U.S. of $25,100 trillion (FRED-5 2024).

21 The fear us that the agency setting prices will have difficulty with optimal pricing. If the price for service is too low in comparison with other services, providers will respond by restricting the too-low priced service. If the price is too set too high without realizing it, then excess profits are generated.

Currently rates are set by Medicare based on American Medical Association (AMA) resource-based relative value weighting based on time, skill, physical effort, stress, and judgment required *plus* overhead for assistance, equipment, and supplies *plus* professional liability. It is then weighted on a national average and then adjusted to locality (ASHA 2024).

While this weighting may continue to make sense, the national average may be in danger of having no market-driven basis because it could become a self-perpetuating loop on a price that had no real market or cost basis in the first place. One could have audible costs, like the time and material contracting and audit system of DoD but this would come with a cost — and that cost could be minimized by only paying for audit system for select providers that would serve as a market-based sample.

22 The poverty rate is defined by how many people are in the household. If we take the census of a 132,000 families in poverty, over 100,000 worked. Looking at the number working over 27 hours a week making $30,000 to $34,999 (Census Bureau-3 2024). The four person household poverty limit of $32,150 for 2023 falls almost in the middle. Anyone working full time making over $29,739 will get a tax break that will push them over the $32,150 limit. To estimate the percentage I allocate half of 4,095 families in this bracket. This is 1.6% of the households. The poverty rate in 2023 was 11.1%. Moving this 1.6% of 11.1% out of poverty give an estimate of 10.9%.

For the childcare estimate, I use the added income for children of about $23,000 for a working household and apply it to the Census survey of family size. Of course, the childcare plan supplement varies by number of children not family size, so this should be seen as a rough estimate. This overlaps with the tax calculation above as well. The estimate results in a reduction in poverty rate of 1%.

Note: This was added after a comment from a Kirkus review.

23 A Value Added Tax (VAT) is a transaction tax. It is essentially a sales tax imposed on the business who sells goods and services to the consumer. Unlike the U.S. Sales Tax, the consumer does not see the tax, only a higher price. It is a regressive tax, like sales tax, so that any positive VAT tax would be counter productive to the American Worker.

24 Communities are beginning to protest server farms, one reason being the "hum" from fan noise. The promise of economic development in a community is short lived — once the server farm is built, very few employees are needed to maintain it compared to the capital cost.

25 The three digit area codes are part of the North American Numbering Plan (NANP) which includes Canada, Mexico, and the Caribbean. It would be a good idea to restrict assigning numbers for the area covered by the NANP.

REFERENCES

Any reference with "(Accessed" and a date) is a reference which is undated.

Ababa, Addis. "Giving the poor a wodge of cash is better than dripping it out." *Economist*. December 7, 2023.
- https://www.economist.com/middle-east-and-africa/2023/12/07/giving-the-poor-a-wodge-of-cash-is-better-than-dripping-it-out •

Abrams, Joel. "Almost no one uses Bitcoin as currency, new data proves. It's actually more like gambling." *The Conversation*. June 22, 2023.
- https://theconversation.com/almost-no-one-uses-bitcoin-as-currency-new-data-proves-its-actually-more-like-gambling-207909# •

Airlines of America. "New Polling Show Consumer Highly Value Airline Credit Card Points." 2022.
- https://www.airlines.org/news-update/new-polling-shows-consumers-highly-value-airline-credit-card-points/#: •

Airport and Airway Trust Fund (AATF). "Fact Sheet." May 2023.
- https://www.faa.gov/sites/faa.gov/files/AATF_Fact_Sheet_2023.pdf•

Aked, Michael, Jim Masturso. "Record Low Costs to Trade!" *Research Affairs*. November 2016.
- https://www.researchaffiliates.com/publications/articles/581_record_low_costs_to_trade •

Ambarian, Johnathan. "Montana to close housing voucher waiting list." KTVH. August 2, 2024.
- https://www.ktvh.com/news/montana-to-close-housing-voucher-waiting-list •

Amadeo, Kimberly. "Role of Derivatives in Creating Mortgage Crisis. *The Balance*. October 2021.
- https://www.thebalancemoney.com/role-of-derivatives-in-creating-mortgage-crisis-3970477 •

Androus, Amanda Burreri. "Here's How Much Your Healthcare Costs Will Rise as You Age." *Registered Nursing*. September 4, 2024.
- https://www.registerednursing.org/articles/healthcare-costs-by-age/ •

Archer, Daine. "Medicare Is More Efficient Than Private Insurance." *Health Affairs*. September 20, 2011.
- https://www.healthaffairs.org/do/10.1377/forefront.20110920.013390/ •

Argyle Haus of Apparel. "Top 3 Factors: Made in USA vs China Made Clothing." July 2018.
- https://www.argylehaus.com/usa-made-china-made-top-3-factors/ •

ARRP Tax Calculator. (Accessed 12/22/2024)
- https://www.aarp.org/money/taxes/1040-tax-calculator/ •

ASHA. "Calculating Medicare Fee Schedule Rate." American Speech-Language-Hearing Assoc. (Accessed 12/9/2024).
- https://www.asha.org/practice/reimbursement/medicare/calculating-medicare-fee-schedule-rates/ •

Bahadori. Hamid (Automobile Club of Southern California). "A Brief History of Roads." Orange County Transportation Authority. February 25, 2008.
- https://www.octa.net/pdf/022508/trans_fund.pdf •

Baker, Christopher. "The Horrors of Child Labor in Dicken's Time." *Hartford Stage*. 2024.
- https://www.hartfordstage.org/stagenotes/acc12/child-labor •

Banerji, Gunjan. "Why Wall Street Loves Poker." *Wall Street Journal.* September 7-8, 2024. p. B-1.
- https://www.wsj.com/public/resources/documents/SskW9BECxkxudA2Y6ZCC-WSJNewsPaper-9-7-2024.pdf •

Banthin, Jessica, Sarah Masi, "CBO's Estimate of the Net Budgetary Impact of the Affordable Care Act's Health Insurance Coverage Provisions Has Not Changed Much Over Time." Congressional Budget Office. May 14. 2013
- https://www.cbo.gov/publication/44176 •

Berry, Wendell. *The Unsettling of America: Culture & Agriculture. Berkeley: Counter Point.* 1977

Berwick. Angus. Ben Foldy. "A Crypto Shadow Dollar Undermines Sanctions." *Wall Street Journal.* September 11, 2024.
- https://www.wsj.com/public/resources/documents/J6sxNf3fCAZ2aqqmFom5-WSJNewsPaper-9-11-2024.pdf •

Beyer, Don. "Decades of Manufacturing Decline and Outsourcing Left U.S. Supply Chains Vulnerable to Distribution." Joint Economic Committee. U.S. Senate. Undated (Accessed 9/21/2024).
- https://www.jec.senate.gov/public/_cache/files/94bf8985-1e87-438b-9a3a-e3334489dd30/background-on-issues-in-us-manufacturing-and-supply-chains-final.pdf •

Biden, President Joe. "FACT SHEET: President Biden Announces New Workforce Hubs to Train and Connect American Workers to Good Jobs Created by the President's Investing in America Agenda." White House Press Release. April 24, 2024.
- https://www.whitehouse.gov/briefing-room/statements-releases/2024/04/25/fact-sheet-president-biden-announces-new-workforce-hubs-to-train-and-connect-american-workers-to-good-jobs-created-by-the-presidents-investing-in-america-agenda/ •

Bjera, Alan. September 13, 2011. "How Goldman Sachs started the food speculation frenzy." *Ecologist.* September 13, 2011.
- https://theecologist.org/2011/sep/13/how-goldman-sachs-started-food-speculation-frenzy •

BLS-1. "A look at manufacturing jobs on National Manufacturing Day." US Bureau of Labor Statistics. TED: Economics Daily. October 6, 2023.
- https://www.bls.gov/opub/ted/2023/a-look-at-manufacturing-jobs-on-national-manufacturing-day.htm •

BLS-2. "Usual Weekly Earnings of Wage and Salary Workers Second Quarter 2024." July 17, 2024.
- https://www.bls.gov/news.release/pdf/wkyeng.pdf •

BLS-3 "Employer Costs for Employee Compensation. March 2024". USDL-24-1172. US Bureau of Labor Statistics. June 18, 2024.
- https://www.bls.gov/news.release/pdf/ecec.pdf •

BLS-4. "Data Bases. Tables & Calculators by Subject: Employment. Hours. and Earnings from the Current Employment Statistics survey (National)". US Bureau of Labor Statistics. Aug 18, 2024.
- https://data.bls.gov/timeseries/CES3000000001 •

BLS-5 "Employment Characteristics of Families — 2023." US Bureau of Labor Statistics. April 24, 202.4.
- https://www.bls.gov/news.release/pdf/famee.pdf •

BLS-6. Table A-1/ Employment status of the civilian population by sex and age." US Bureau of Labor Statistics. August 2024.
- https://www.bls.gov/news.release/empsit.t01.htm •

BLS--7. "Workman's Comp." US Bureau of Labor Statistics. Spotlight On Statistics. 2024.
- https://www.bls.gov/spotlight/2016/workplace-injuries-and-illnesses-and-employer-costs-for-work-

ers-compensation/ •

BLS-8. "Table B-8. Average hourly and weekly earnings of production and nonsupervisory employees on private nonfarm payrolls by industry sector. seasonally adjusted." US Bureau of Labor Statistics. April 24, 2024.
• https://www.bls.gov/news.release/empsit.t24.htm#ces_table8.f.1 •

BLS-9. May 2023 National Industry-Specific Occupational Employment and Wage Estimates." US Bureau of Labor Statistics. Occupational Employment and Wage Statistics. May 2023.
• https://www.bls.gov/oes/2023/may/naics2_31-33.htm#45-0000 •

BLS-10. "Comparing characteristics and selected expenditures of dual- and single-income households with children" September 2020.
• https://www.bls.gov/opub/mlr/2020/article/comparing-characteristics-and-selected-expenditures-of-dual-and-single-income-households-with-children.htm •

BLS-11. "Productivity and Costs, Third Quarter 2024, Revised." 2024
• https://www.bls.gov/news.release/prod2.nr0.htm •

BLS-12. "Productivity Measures: Business Sector and Major Subsectors: Concepts." (Accessed 1/9/2025).
• https://www.bls.gov/opub/hom/msp/concepts.htm#Laborinput •

Brandt, Loran et al. "Chapter 9 Industrializing in China." Rourke. Kevin and Jeffrey Williamson (Ed.). Oxford: Oxford University Press: *The Spread of Modern Industry to the Periphery since 1871*, 2017

Brook. Robert A. "Measuring the Burden of Administrative Costs." before the Committee on Health. Education. Labor. and Pensions United States Senate. July 31, 2018.

Bureau of Economic Analysis. "Gross Domestic Product." Bureau of Economic Analysis. US Dept. of Commerce. Undated. (Accessed 9/12/2024).
• https://www.bea.gov/system/files/2020-04/GDP-Education-by-BEA.pdf •

Burns, Alice. Jaeger Nelson. "Policy Alternatives for Long-Term Services and Supports." Congressional Budget Office. November 19–2021.
• https://www.cbo.gov/system/files/2021-11/57451-LTSS.pdf •

Butler SM. "The Future of the Affordable Care Act: Reassessment and Revision." *JAMA*. 316(5):495–497. 2016
• doi:10.1001/jama.2016.9881 •

Campbell. Tessa. Jake Safane. "Average Stock Return: A Historical Perspective and Future Outlook. *Business Insider*. September 16, 2024.
• https://www.businessinsider.com/personal-finance/investing/average-stock-market-return •

Cannon, Michael. "End the Tax Exclusion for Employer-Sponsored Health Insurance." Cato Institute, Policy Analysis No. 928. May 24, 2022.
• https://www.cato.org/policy-analysis/end-tax-exclusion-employer-sponsored-health-insurance-return-1-trillion-workers-who •

Cantrell. Sue. Corrie Commission. "Outcomes over outputs: Why productivity is no longer the metric that mat-ters most." *Dolittle Insights*. Quarter 1, 2024.
• https://www2.deloitte.com/us/en/insights/topics/talent/measuring-productivity.html •

CAP20-1. "Excess Administrative Costs Burden the U.S. Health Care System." Center for American Progress. April 8, 2019.
• https://www.americanprogress.org/article/excess-administrative-costs-burden-u-s-health-care-system/ •

CAP20-2. "Data on Poverty in the United States." Center for American Progress. 2024.
• https://www.americanprogress.org/data-view/poverty-data/ •

Caporal, Jack. "The House Flipping Statistics Investors Should Know in 2024." Motley Fool. September 19–2024.
• https://www.fool.com/research/house-flipping-statistics/ •

Care. "This is how much child care costs in 2024." Care∎ January 17, 2024.
• https://www.care.com/c/how-much-does-child-care-cost/#h-toddler-child-care-cost-per-week •

Caring Support Blog. "Pros And Cons Of Healthcare In Canada: A Closer Look." November 2, 2023.
• https://www.caringsupport.com/blog/advantages-and-disadvantages-of-canadas-healthcare-system •

CBO-1. *Options for Reducing the Deficit. 2023 to 2023*. Vol. 1: Large Reductions. Congressional Budget Office. December 2022.
• https://www.cbo.gov/system/files/2022-12/58164-budget-options-large-effects.pdf •

CBO-2. *Options for Reducing the Deficit. 2023 to 2023*. Vol. 2 Smaller Reductions. Congressional Budget Office. December 2022.
• https://www.cbo.gov/system/files/2022-12/58163-budget-options-small-effects.pdf •

CBO-3. *Options for Reducing Deficit*. Congressional Budget Office. 2019.
• https://www.cbo.gov/system/files/2019-06/54667-budgetoptions-2.pdf •

CBO-4. "How CBO Analyzes the Costs of Proposals for Single-Payer Health Care Systems That Are Based on Medicare's Fee-for-Service Program." CBO's Single-Payer Health Care Systems Team, Congressional Budget Office. December 2020.
• https://www.cbo.gov/system/files/2020-12/56811-Single-Payer.pdf •

CBO-5. "Federal Subsidies for Health Insurance: 2023 to 2032 ." Congressional Budget Office. September 2023.
• https://www.cbo.gov/system/files/2023-09/59273-health-coverage.pdf •

CBO-6. "The Prices That Commercial Health Insurers and Medicare Pay for Hospitals' and Physicians' Services ." Congressional Budget Office. January 2022.
• https://www.cbo.gov/system/files/2022-01/57422-medical-prices.pdf •

CBO-7. "The 2020 Long-Term Budget Outlook." Congressional Budget Office. September 2020.
• https://www.cbo.gov/system/files/2020-09/56516-LTBO.pdf •

CBO-8. *Options for Reducing the Deficit: 2025 to 2034*. Congressional Budget Office. December 2024.
• https://www.cbo.gov/system/files/2024-12/60557-budget-options.pdf

CBO-9. Letter: Douglas Elmendorf, Director to Senator Orrin Hatch, in reference to the Wall Street Trading and Speculators Tax Act H.R. 3313 or S. 1787. Congressional Budget Office. December 12, 2011.
• https://www.cbo.gov/sites/default/files/112th-congress-2011-2012/reports/12-12-2011_Hatch_Letter.pdf •

Cboe-1. "U.S. Equities Market Volume Summary."December 20, 2024.
• https://www.cboe.com/us/equities/market_statistics/ •

Cboe-2. "Historic Market Volume Data." Market_History_2024.csv (Accessed 1/10/2025).
• https://www.cboe.com/us/equities/market_statistics/historical_market_volume/: •

Census Bureau-1. "HINC-04. Presence of Children Under 18 Years old--Households. by Total Money Income. Type of Household. Race and Hispanic Origin of Householder." U.S. Census Bureau 2023.
• https://www.census.gov/data/tables/time-series/demo/income-poverty/cps-hinc/hinc-04.html#par_list_10 •

References

Census Bureau-2. Adam Gundy, et al."Medical Expenditure Panel Survey – Insurance Component Shows 86% of Private-Sector Employees Worked for Establishments that Offered Health Insurancer." U.S. Census Bureau, February 29, 2024.

Census Bureau-3."HINC-01. Selected Characteristics of Households by Total Money Income.." U.S. Census Bureau, April 21, 2024.
• https://www.census.gov/data/tables/time-series/demo/income-poverty/cps-hinc/hinc-01.html •

Center on Budget and Policy Priorities-1. "Policy Basics: The Earned Income Tax Credit." April 8, 2023.
• https://www.cbpp.org/research/policy-basics-the-earned-income-tax-credit •

Center on Budget and Policy Priorities-2. "Policy Basics: State Earned Income Tax Credit." July 24, 2024.
• https://www.cbpp.org/research/policy-basics-the-earned-income-tax-credit •

Center on Budget and Policy Priorities-3. "Policy Basics: Understanding the Social Security Trust Funds." October 13, 2021.
• https://www.cbpp.org/research/social-security/understanding-the-social-security-trust-funds-0 •

CFTC, "Transaction Dollar Volume by Cleared Status (Millions of USD) (Single-Count) - 09/27/2024." Commodity Futures Trading Commission. 2024.
• https://www.cftc.gov/MarketReports/SwapsReports/L1TransDollarVolCS.html •

Chew, W. Bruce. "No-Nonsense Guide to Measuring." *Harvard Business Review*. January 1988.
• https://hbr.org/1988/01/no-nonsense-guide-to-measuring-productivity •

Chisholm, Shirley. *Unbought and Unbossed*. New York: Harper Collins. 1970.

CMS. "NHE Fact Sheet." Centers for Medicare and Medicaid Services. 2023.
• https://www.cms.gov/data-research/statistics-trends-and-reports/national-health-expenditure-data/nhe-fact-sheet# •

Cohen, Ariel. "AI Is Pushing The World Toward An Energy Crisis" *Forbes*. May 23, 2024.
• https://www.forbes.com/sites/arielcohen/2024/05/23/ai-is-pushing-the-world-towards-an-energy-crisis/# •

CoinMarketCap. "Today's Cryptocurrency Prices by Market Cap." (Accessed 12/26/2024).
• https://coinmarketcap.com •

Collyer, Sophie, et al. "Children Left Behind by the Child Tax Credit in 2022." *Poverty and Social Policy Brief*. Vol. 7. No. 4. September 12, 2023.
• www.povertycenter.columbia.edu/publication/2023/children-left-behind-by-the-child-tax-credit-in-2022 •

Committee on the Consequences of Uninsurance. *Hidden Cost. Values Lost. Uninsurance in America*. Washington DC: Instituted of Medicine of the National Academies of Science. 2003.
• https://nap.nationalacademies.org/read/10719/chapter/1 •

Commonwealth Fund-1. Miriam Blümel, Reinhard Busse. International Health Care System Profiles, Germany." (Accessed 1/2/2025).
• https://www.commonwealthfund.org/international-health-policy-center/countries/germany •

Commonwealth Fund-2 . Isabell Sturny. International Health Care System Profiles, Switzerland." (Accessed 1/2/2025).
• https://www.commonwealthfund.org/international-health-policy-center/countries/switzerland •

CRS. "Attaching a Price to Greenhouse Gas Emissions with a Carbon Tax or Emissions Fee: Considerations and Potential Impacts " R4625. Congressional Research Service. March 19–2019.
• https://crsreports.congress.gov/product/pdf/R/R45625 •

Cox, Cynthia. Jared Ortaliz. Emma Wager. Krutika Amin. Chapter: "Health Care Costs and Affordability." *KFF's Health Policy 101*. Edited by Drew Altman. KFF. May 28, 2024.
• https://www.kff.org/health-policy-101-health-care-costs-and-affordability/ •

CRS. "How Did COVID-19 Unemployment Insurance Benefits Impact Consumer Spending and Employment?" Congressional Research Service. June 24, 2022.
• https://crsreports.congress.gov/product/pdf/IF/IF12143#: •

Crypto.com. "How Much Energy Does Bitcoin Consume?" Undated (Accessed 10/6/2024).
• https://crypto.com/bitcoin/bitcoin-energy-consumption#: •

Crair, Ben. "The Secret Economic Lives of Animals." *Bloomberg*. August 1, 2017.
• https://www.bloomberg.com/features/2017-biological-markets/ AND • • https://drive.google.com/file/d/0B_l9YgPTHVjuV0ZFOWpTaXJlcVk •

Data Team Economist. "Are women paid less than men for the same work?" *Economist*. August 1, 2017.
• https://www.economist.com/graphic-detail/2017/08/01/are-women-paid-less-than-men-for-the-same-work •

Daugherty, Greg. "Gender and Income Inequality: History and Statistics. Investopedia. March 27, 2024.
• https://www.investopedia.com/history-gender-wage-gap-america-5074898# •

Defense Health Program. "Fiscal Year (FY) 2024 President's Budget." March 2023.
• https://comptroller.defense.gov/Portals/45/Documents/defbudget/fy2024/budget_justification/pdfs/09_Defense_Health_Program/00-DHP_Vols_I_II_and_III_PB24.pdf •

Drum, Kevin. "Chart of the Day: Housing Prices Since WWII." *Moth.er Jones*. August 24, 2010.
• https://www.motherjones.com/kevin-drum/2010/08/chart-day-housing-prices-wwii/ •

EPA, "Supplementary Material for the Regulatory Impact Analysis for the Supplemental Proposed Rulemaking. 'Standards of Performance for New. Reconstructed. and Modified Sources and Emissions Guidelines for Existing Sources: Oil and Natural Gas Sector Climate Review'." Docket ID No. EPA-HQ-OAR-2021-0317 (Draft). September 2022.
• https://www.epa.gov/system/files/documents/2022-11/epa_scghg_report_draft_0.pdf •

Erwin, Sandra. "Pentagon greenlights $140 billion ICBM program despite cost overruns" *Space News*. July 8, 2024.
• https://spacenews.com/pentagon-greenlights-140-billion-icbm-program-despite-cost-overruns/ •

Evans, Joseph. "Modern supply side economics: A new consensus?" *IPPR Progressive Review*. January 9, 2024.
• https://www.ippr.org/articles/modern-supply-side-economics-a-new-consensus •

Federal Hospital Insurance Board of Trustees. 2024 Annual Report of the Boards of Trustees of the Federal Hospital Insurance and Federal Supplementary Insurance Trust Funds. May 6, 2024.
• https://www.cms.gov/oact/tr/2024 •

Federal Reserve History. "Stock Market Crash of 1929." Federal Reserve. Undated (Accessed 9/202024).
• https://www.federalreservehistory.org/essays/stock-market-crash-of-1929 •

Ferando, Jason. "Gross Domestic Product (GD_ Formula and How to Use It." Investopedia. June 3, 2024.
• https://www.investopedia.com/terms/g/gdp.asp#: •

References

Fermano, Jason. "Derivatives: Types. Considerations .and Pros and Cons." Investopedia. May 31, 2024.
• https://www.investopedia.com/terms/d/derivative.asp •

Fleming, Michael. "Measuring Treasury Market Liquidity." Federal Reserve Bank. New York. September 2003.
• https://www.newyorkfed.org/medialibrary/media/research/epr/03v09n3/0309flempdf.pdf •

FRED-1. Median Sales Price of a House Sold in The United States." FRED Economic Data. Federal Reserve Saint Louis. 2024.
• https://fred.stlouisfed.org/series/MSPUS •

FRED-2. "Hours worked by full-time and part-time employees". FRED Economic Data. FED Saint Louis. October 26. .2023.
• https://fred.stlouisfed.org/series/B4701C0A222NBEA •

FRED-3. "Average Hourly Earnings of All Employees. Manufacturing". FRED Economic Data. FED Saint Louis. October 26. .2023
• https://fred.stlouisfed.org/series/CES3000000003 •

FRED-4. "Total Wages and Salaries". FRED Economic Data. FED Saint Louis. October 26. .2023
• https://fred.stlouisfed.org/series/BA06RC1A027NBEA •

FRED-5. "Total Personal Income". FRED Economic Data. FED Saint Louis. November 27, 2024
• https://fred.stlouisfed.org/series/PI •

FRED-6. "Consumer Price Index for All Urban Customers: Airline Fares in U.S. City Average." FRED Economic Data. FED Saint Louis. December 11, 2024
• https://fred.stlouisfed.org/series/CUSR0000SETG01 •

Gibson M. Thomson H. Banas K. Lutje V. et al. "Welfare-to-work interventions and their effects on the mental and physical health of lone parents and their children." Cochrane Database Syst Rev. 2(2):CD009820. February 26, 2018. doi: 10.1002/14651858.CD009820.pub3.

Galvani AP, Parpia AS, et al. "Improving the prognosis of health care in the USA." *Lancet*. February 12, 2020.
• doi: 10.1016/S0140-6736(19)33019-3 •

Glamsmeier Amy and MT. "Living Wage Calculator." MIT. 2024.
• https://livingwage.mit.edu/states/31 •

Global Data. "Number of Households with Children in the United States." November 2022.
• https://www.globaldata.com/data-insights/macroeconomic/number-of-households-with-children-in-the-united-states-2137583/ •

Gómez-Jorge. Fabiola and Eloísa Díaz-Garrido. "The relation between Self-Esteem and Productivity: An analysis is higher education institutions." *Frontiers of Psychology* Vol. 31. January 10, 2023.
• https://www.frontiersin.org/journals/psychology/articles/10.3389/fpsyg.2022.1112437/full •

Gwartney, James. "Supply-Side Economics." EconLib. Undated. (Accessed 10/9/2024).
• https://www.econlib.org/library/Enc/SupplySideEconomics.html •

Griffin, David K. et al. "A Comparison of Self-Esteem and Job Satisfaction of Adults with Mild Mental Retar-dation in Sheltered Workshops and Supported Employment." *Education and Training in Mental Retardation and Developmental Disabilitie*s. vol. 31. no. 2, 1996. pp. 142–50.
• http://www.jstor.org/stable/23879130. •

Grote, Martin. Jean François Wen."How to Design and Implement Property Tax Reforms." International Monetary Fund. September 2024.
• https://www.imf.org/en/Publications/imf-how-to-notes/Issues/2024/09/19/How-to-Design-and-Implement-Property-Tax-Reforms-555103 •

Habitat for Humanity. "Habitat for Humanity International Evidence Brief: Wealth Building." 20-78904/PDF.US/12-2020. (Accessed 9/12/2024).
• https://www.habitat.org/sites/default/files/Evidence-Brief_Wealth-building-for-homeowners.pdf •

Harris, Benjamin. "What Changes in the Mortgage Deduction Would Mean for Home Prices." Tax Policy Center, June 5, 2013.
• https://taxpolicycenter.org/taxvox/what-changes-mortgage-deduction-would-mean-home-prices •

Harper, Kelly. "Supply-Side Economics: What You Need to Know" *Investopedia*. September 11, 2023.
• https://www.investopedia.com/articles/05/011805.asp •

Hazen, Tamatha. "Average child care & daycare costs." trustedcare. February 1, 2024
• https://trustedcare.com/costs/child-care-cost# •

Health Care Value Hub. "Excess Administrative Spending in Healthcare: Significant Savings Possible." Research Brief no. 30, November 2018.
• https://www.healthcarevaluehub.org/advocate-resources/publications/excess-administrative-spending-healthcare-significant-savings-possible •

HHS. *Fiscal Year 2025 Budget in Brief*. U.S. Dept. of Health and Human Services. 2024.
• https://www.hhs.gov/sites/default/files/fy-2025-budget-in-brief.pdf •

Horowitze, Alex. "How Housing Costs Drive Levels of Homelessness." Pew Research. August 22, 2023.
• https://www.pewtrusts.org/en/research-and-analysis/articles/2023/08/22/how-housing-costs-drive-levels-of-homelessness •

HTS. "Harmonized Tariff Schedule. 2024 HTS Rev. 8." U.S. International Trade Organization. August 12, 2024.
• https://hts.usitc.gov •

Hofbauer, Jachim, et al. "Cost and Time Overruns for Major Defense Acquisition Programs." Center for Strategic & International Studies, CSIS-AM-11-163. April 2011.
• https://dair.nps.edu/bitstream/123456789/2493/1/CSIS-AM-11-163.pdf •

HUD. "Housing Choice Vouchers Fact Sheet." U.S. Department of Housing and Urban Development. (Accessed 10/4/2024).
* https://www.hud.gov/topics/housing_choice_voucher_program_section_8 •

Hussien, Omar. "Stock Transfer Taxes in the Modern Age." Stetson Business Law Review. 2024.
• https://www.stetson.edu/law/business-law-review/media/Hussein.HC.sheridan.final.2%20Linked%20in%20post%20with%20logo.pdf •

ICE. "Historical Monthly Volumes: ICE Futures U.S." 2024.
• https://www.ice.com/report/8 •

Insurance Information Institute. "Facts + Statistics: Workplace Safety/Workers Comp." 2023.
• https://www.iii.org/fact-statistic/facts-statistics-workplace-safety-workers-comp •

IRS-1. "SOI Tax Stats - Individual Statistal tables by filing status." Internal Revenue Service. 2024. Downloaded Excel Spreadsheets: Table 1.3 - 2021 Table 2.2 - 2022. Table 2.4 - 2017.
• https://www.irs.gov/statistics/soi-tax-stats-individual-Statistal-tables-by-filing-status •

IRS-2. "Statistics for Tax Returns with the Earned Income Tax Credit (EITC)." Internal Revenue Service. 2024.
- https://www.eitc.irs.gov/eitc-central/statistics-for-tax-returns-with-eitc/statistics-for-tax-returns-with-the-earned-income •

IRS-3. "Historical Highlights for the IRS." Internal Revenue Service. (Accessed 12/27/2024).
- https://www.irs.gov/newsroom/historical-highlights-of-the-irs# •

IRTA. "The Barter and Trade Industry." International Reciprocal Trade Association. (Accessed 9/8/2024).
- https://www.irta.com/about/the-barter-and-trade-industry/ •

iTeleCenter. "How to get a US phone number from outside the US (2024)" March 11, 2024.
- https://www.itelecenter.com/blog/how-to-get-a-us-phone-number •

Johnson, Micah. Sanjay Kishor. Donald M. Berwick. "Medicare-for-All: An Analysis Of Key Policy Issues." *Health Affairs*. Vol. 39:1. January 2020.
- https://www.healthaffairs.org/doi/10.1377/hlthaff.2019.01040 •

Kelly, Michael. "The 1992 Campaign: The Democrats -- Clinton and Bush Compete to Be Champion of Change; Democrat Fights Perceptions of Bush Gain." *New York Times*. October 31, 1992.
- https://www.nytimes.com/1992/10/31/us/1992-campaign-democrats-clinton-bush-compete-be-champion-change-democrat-fights.html •

Kenton, Will. "What Is Productivity and How to Measure It." Investopedia. June 26, 2024.
- https://www.investopedia.com/terms/p/productivity.asp •

Keynes, John Maynard. "National Self-Sufficiency." *The Yale Review* Vol. 22. no. 4. June 1933.
- http://gesd.free.fr/knat33.pdf •

KFF-1. "Average Marketplace Premiums by Metal Tier. 2018-2024." KFF. 2024.
- https://www.kff.org/affordable-care-act/state-indicator/average-marketplace-premiums-by-metal-tier/ •

KFF-2. "Total Medicaid Spending." KFF. 2024.
- https://www.kff.org/affordable-care-act/state-indicator/average-monthly-advance-premium-tax-credit-aptc •

KFF-3 "2024 Employer Health Benefits Survey." KFF. 2024.
- https://www.kff.org/report-section/ehbs-2024-summary-of-findings/ •

KFF-4 "Employer-Sponsored Health Insurance 101." KFF. May 28, 2024.
- https://www.kff.org/health-policy-101-employer-sponsored-health-insurance/ •

KFF-5. "Key Facts on Health Coverage of Immigrants" KFF. September 17, 2023.
- https://www.kff.org/racial-equity-and-health-policy/fact-sheet/key-facts-on-health-coverage-of-immigrants/# •

KFF-6. Prira Chidambram, Alice Burns. "How Many People Use Medicaid Long-Term Services and Supports and How Much Does Medicaid Spend on Those People?" KFF, August 14, 2023.
- https://www.kff.org/medicaid/issue-brief/how-many-people-use-medicaid-long-term-services-and-supports-and-how-much-does-medicaid-spend-on-those-people/ •

KFF-7. J. Cubansk, T.Neuman. "FAQs on Medicare Financing and Trust Fund Solvency" KFF, May 29, 2024.
- https://www.kff.org/medicare/issue-brief/faqs-on-medicare-financing-and-trust-fund-solvency/ •

KFF-8. T.Neuman, et al. "How Much More Than Medicare Do Private Insurers Pay? A Review of the Literature KFF, April 15, 2020.
- https://www.kff.org/medicare/issue-brief/how-much-more-than-medicare-do-private-insurers-pay-a-review-of-the-literature// •

Klein. Danial B. "Turnpikes and Tool Roads in the Nineteenth Century." Economic History Association. February 10. 2008.
• https://eh.net/encyclopedia/turnpikes-and-toll-roads-in-nineteenth-century-america/ •

Klien, Aaron. "What is a financial tax?" Brookings. March 27, 2020.
• https://www.brookings.edu/articles/what-is-a-financial-transaction-tax-2/ •

Kochhar, Rakesh. "The State of the America Middle-class." Pew Research Center. May 31, 2024.
• https://www.pewresearch.org/race-and-ethnicity/2024/05/31/the-state-of-the-american-middle-class/ •

LaFranco, Rob and Chase Peterson-Whithorn (Editors). "The Definitive Ranking of The Wealthiest Americans In 2023." *Forbes*. 2024.
• https://www.forbes.com/forbes-400/# •

Lahart, Justin, Lauren Weber. "Workers, Companies In U.S. Get More Productive." *Wall Street Journal*. January 5, 2025.
• https://www.wsj.com/public/resources/documents/pxiSsSHoDqHv8sAQbSFs-WS-JNewsPaper-1-3-2025.pdf •

Lee, Jin Man. Jin Wook Choi. "The Role of House Flippers in a Boom and Bust Real Estate Market." *The Journal of Economic Asymmetries*. Volume 8. Issue 2, 2011. pp. 91-109.
• https://www.sciencedirect.com/science/article/abs/pii/S1703494912302231 •

Liu-1. Jodi L. et al. "An Assessment of the New York Health Act. A Single-Payer Option for New York State. RAND Corporation. August 2018.
• https://www.rand.org/pubs/research_reports/RR2424.html •

Liu-2. Jodi L. "Exploring Single-Payer Alternatives for Health Care Reform." RAND Corporation. August 2016.
• https://www.rand.org/pubs/rgs_dissertations/RGSD375.html •

Liu-3. Jodi L. Christine Elbner. "National Health Spending Estimates Under Medicare-for-All." RAND Corporation. August 10, 2019.
• https://www.rand.org/pubs/research_reports/RR3106.html •

Levin, Matt. "Authors Guild to offer "Human Authored" label on books to compete with AI." Author's Guild. October 7, 2024.
• https://www.marketplace.org/2024/10/07/authors-guild-human-authored-label-ai/ •

Lexington Law. "50 important welfare statistics for 2023." Lexington Law, Salt Lake City. April 10, 2023.
• https://www.lexingtonlaw.com/blog/finance/welfare-statistics.html •

Lieberman, M.B., Kang, J. "How to measure company productivity using value-added: A focus on Pohang Steel (POSCO)." *Asia Pacific J Manage* 25, 209–224, 2008.
• https://doi.org/10.1007/s10490-007-9081-0 •

Liberto, Daniel. "5 Reasons Why Supply-Side Economics Does Not Work." Investopedia. July 31., 2024.
• https://www.investopedia.com/supply-side-economics-6755346 •

Long Term Trends. "Home Price to Median Household Income Ratio." May 31, 2024.
• https://www.longtermtrends.net/home-price-median-annual-income-ra-tio/# •

LaMont, Lindsey. "The True Cost of Spam and Scam Calls in America" *true*caller. March 12, 2024.
• https://www.truecaller.com/blog/insights/the-true-cost-of-spam-and-scam-calls-in-america •

Lawder, David, Andrea Shalal. "Yellen rebrands Biden economic agenda as 'modern supply-side economics'." Reuters. January 21, 2022. https://www.reuters.com/business/yellen-rebrands-biden-economic-agenda-modern-supply-side-economics-2022-01-21/

Lysandrou, Photis. "Why the European Commission is Wrong to Push for a European Financial Transactions Tax." *Tidsskreiftet Polilik*.16:4. December 11, 2013. pp. 52-25. https://doi.org/10.7146/politik.v16i4.27562

Mad Men. Created by: Matthew Winer. Perf. Jon Hamm. Elisabeth Moss. TV Series. AMC. now on Amazon Prime. 2007-2012

Malone, Thomas. "Why we need a 'Digital WPA' similar to the Depression-era Works Progress Administration." *The Hill*. May 5, 2020.
• https://thehill.com/opinion/technology/495943-why-we-need-a-digital-wpa-similar-to-the-depression-era-works-progress/ •

Martin, Roger. "What Economists Get Wrong About Measuring Productivity." *Harvard Business Review*. September 14, 2012.
• https://hbr.org/2012/09/what-economists-get-wrong-about-measuring-productivity •

McGrath. Ellen. "Self-Esteem at Work." *Psychology Today*. October 1, 2001.
• https://www.psychologytoday.com/us/articles/200110/self-esteem-work •

Mental Health America. "Development of Employment Services for Adults in Recovery from Mental Health and Substance Use Conditions." December 31, 2022.
• https://mhanational.org/issues/development-employment-services-adults-recovery-mental-health-and-substance-use-conditions •

Meyer, Susan. "Average length of homeownership: Americans spend less than 12 years in one home." *the Zebra*. March 11, 2024.
• https://www.thezebra.com/resources/home/average-length-of-homeownership/•

Miller, Colin, Anna Tyger. "The Impact of a Financial Transaction Tax." Tax Foundation. January 23, 2020. https://taxfoundation.org/research/all/federal/financial-transaction-tax/

Mixon, Scott. "U.S. Experience with Futures Transactions Taxes:Effects in a Highly Intermediated Market." Office of Chief Economist, Commodity Trading Commission. January 2016.
• https://www.cftc.gov/sites/default/files/idc/groups/public/@economicanalysis/documents/file/oce_futurestranstax.pdf •

Montevirgen. Kar. "Commission-free stock trading: Is there a catch?" *Britannica Money*. (Accessed 9/22/2024).
• https://www.britannica.com/money/commission-free-trading-definition •

Nash, Jennifer "Middle-class Hourly Wages as of August 2024." VettaFi Advisor Perspectives. September 11, 2024.
• https://www.advisorperspectives.com/dshort/updates/2024/09/11/middle-class-hourly-wages-as-of-august-2024•

National Child Labor Committee Collection. Library of Congress. 1904.
• https://www.loc.gov/pictures/collection/nclc/background.html •

National Employment Project. "Benefit Amounts." Policy Advocacy Brief. November 2023.
• https://www.nelp.org/app/uploads/2023/11/Policy-Advocacy-Brief-Benefit-Amounts-11-2023.pdf •

Neilsen, Eric. "Zero-Sum Game." Region Focus. Richmond Fed. Spring 2005.
• https://www.richmondfed.org/-/media/RichmondFedOrg/publications/research/econ_focus/2005/spring/pdf/jargon_alert.pdf •

Nelson, Jaeger. "Economic Effects of Five Illustrative Single-Payer Health Care Systems." Working Paper. Congressional Budget Office. February 2022.
• https://www.cbo.gov/system/files/2022-02/57637-Single-Payer-Systems.pdf •

New American Economy. "Undocumented Immigrants." (Accessed 10/9/2024).
• https://www.newamericaneconomy.org/issues/undocumented-immigrants/ •

New Jersey Dept. of Labor and Workforce Development. "Temporary Disability Insurance Workload inm 2019, Summary Report." August 2020.
• https://www.nj.gov/labor/myleavebenefits/assets/pdfs/TDI%20Report%20for%202019.pdf •

New York State Department of Taxation and Finance. "Stock Transfer Tax." (Accessed 9/22/2024).
• https://www.tax.ny.gov/bus/stock/stktridx.htm •

NFTEvening. "Electricity Costs to Mine 1 Bitcoin at Home, Around the World." September 23, 2024.
• https://nftevening.com/bitcoin-mining-cost/# •

Noë, Ronald and Peter Hammerstein. "Biological markets: supply and demand determine the effect of partner choice in cooperation, mutualism and mating." *Behav Ecol Social Bio.* 35:1-11, 1994.
• https://science.umd.edu/faculty/wilkinson/BIOL608W/Noe&Hammerstein1994BES.pdf •

OECD iLibrary. "Waiting Times for Health Services: Next in Line." Chapter 2, "How Long Are Waiting Lines?" 2024
• https://www.oecd-ilibrary.org/sites/242e3c8c-en/1/3/2/index.html? •

Official Data Foundation Food. "Other Foods Inflation Calculator." (Accessed 9/6/2024).
• https://www.in2013dollars.com/Other-foods/price-inflation/1963-to-2024?amount=1 •

Office of US Trades Representative. "Countries and Regions." (Accessed 9/24/2024).
• https://ustr.gov/countries-regions#: •

OpemSaxCOllege. "The Stock Market Crash pf 1929." OpenStaxCollee and Rice University. 2014. • https://pressbooks-dev.oer.hawaii.edu/ushistory/chapter/the-stock-market-crash-of-1929/ •

O'Malley Katherine. Katherine Miller. Melissa Garrido. "Payers of Long-Term Services and Supports for Veterans." US Dept. of Veterans Affairs. Partnered Evidence-based Policy Resource Center. January 2024.
• https://www.peprec.research.va.gov/PEPRECRESEARCH/docs/Policy_Brief_23_Payers_LTSS.pdf •

Omeokwe, Amara. "Janet Yellen Views Biden Policies as Modernized Supply-Side Economics." *Wall Street Journal,* January 21, 2022.
• https://www.wsj.com/articles/janet-yellen-views-biden-policies-as-modernized-supply-side-economics-11642792184 •

Passel, Jeffery. "What we know about unauthorized immigrants living in the U.S." PEW Research Center. July 22, 2024.
•https://www.pewresearch.org/short-reads/2024/07/22/what-we-know-about-unauthorized-immigrants-living-in-the-us/ •

Paulton, Meridian. "Single-Payer Health Care: Rhetoric Versus Reality." The Heritage Foundatin, No. 3404, April 25, 2019.
• https://www.heritage.org/sites/default/files/2019-04/BG3404.pdf •

Peter G. Peterson Foundation. "Budget Basics Medicaid." Novemeber 13, 2024.
• https://www.pgpf.org/article/budget-explainer-medicaid/ •

Plum|voice. "Where Do Telephone Numbers Come From?" (Accessed 10/3/2024).
• https://www.plumvoice.com/resources/blog/where-do-telephone-numbers-come-from •

Parzs, Sabrina. "Child and Dependent Care Credit Definition. Who Qualifies." Nerd Wallet. January 31, 2024.
• https://www.nerdwallet.com/article/taxes/child-and-dependent-care-tax-credit •

Passel, Jeffery, Jens Krogstad. "What we know about unauthorized immigrants living in the U.S." Pew Research Center. July 22, 2024.
• https://www.pewresearch.org/short-reads/2024/07/22/what-we-know-about-unauthorized-immigrants-living-in-the-us/ •

Pho, Yvon H. "Volunteer Output and the National Accounts: An Empirical Analysis." WP2004-03. Bureau of Economic Analysis. February 20-22, 2004.
• https://www.bea.gov/index.php/system/files/papers/WP2004-3.pdf •

Pine, Ivana, Sarah Gae. "Average cost of childcare in 2023." Bankrate May 29. 2023.
•https://www.bankrate.com/credit-cards/news/average-cost-of-childcare/• .

PNC Insights. "2026 Tax Law Changes: Prepare for TCJA Provisions to Sunset." February 5, 2024.
• https://www.pnc.com/insights/wealth-management/markets-economy/2026-tax-law-changes-prepare-for-TCJA-provisions-to-sunset.html •

Pollin. Robert. et al. "Securities Transaction Taxes for U.S. Financial Markets." *Eastern Economic Journal.* vol. 29. no. 4, 2003. pp. 527–58.
• http://www.jstor.org/stable/40326385. (also: Working Paper Series #20. University of Massachusetts Amherst. October 2002. • https://scholarworks.umass.edu/entities/publication/87b-0fedf-754d-4d44-9cfe-17d0bcf51a98 •

PriceWaterHouseCopper. "China People's Republic of China. Individual - Taxes on personal income." June 28, 2024.
• https://taxsummaries.pwc.com/peoples-republic-of-china/individual/taxes-on-personal-income •

pwc. "Chain People's Republic of. Individual taxes." June 28, 2024.
• https://taxsummaries.pwc.com/peoples-republic-of-china/individual/taxes-on-personal-income •

Qualman, Darrin. "Home grown: 67 years of US and Canadian house size data. Darrin Qualman. May 8, 2018.
• https://www.darrinqualman.com/house-size/ •

Rainey, Michael. "Once Again: The GOP Tax Cuts Are Not Paying for Themselves" *The Financial Times*. March 13, 2019.
• https://www.thefiscaltimes.com/2019/03/13/Once-Again-GOP-Tax-Cuts-Are-Not-Paying-Themselves •

Rassol, Sanam, et al. "Revenue Implications of Tax Cut and Jobs Act Provisions in 2025." Center for Strategic & International Studies. December 19–2024.
• https://www.csis.org/analysis/revenue-implications-tax-cut-and-jobs-act-provisions-2025 •

Reiff, Nathan. "Bidenomics: How Joe Biden's Policies Are Shaping the U.S. Economy." Investopedia. October 31, 2024.
• https://www.investopedia.com/bidenomics-8363974e •

Riis, Jacob. *How the Other Half Lives: Studies among the Tenements of New York*. New York: Charles Scribe's Sons. 1890

Ross University. "US vs. Canadian Healthcare: What is The Difference?" May 11, 2021.
• https://medical.rossu.edu/about/blog/us-vs-canadian-healthcare •

Rozo, Matt. "What's Changing in 2025 with Cannabis: A Look at Federal Legalization Efforts." *The Mercury News*. January 10, 2025.
• https://www.mercurynews.com/2025/01/10/whats-changing-in-2025-with-cannabis-a-look-at-federal-legalization-efforts/ •

Ryan, John A. "The Ethics of Speculation." The International Journal of Ethics. Vol. 12:3. April 1902, pp. 273-416.
• https://www.journals.uchicago.edu/doi/epdf/10.1086/intejethi.12.3.2376347 •

Safe Gaurd Global. "Top 10 manufacturing countries in the world in 2024.". August 28, 2024.
- https://www.safeguardglobal.com/resources/top-10-manufacturing-countries-in-the-world/ •

Samuelson, Robert J. "Debunking the Two-Earner Family Myth." January 24, 1997.
- https://www.latimes.com/archives/la-xpm-1997-01-24-me-21204-story.html •

Seth, Shobhit. "The World of High Frequency Trading." September 16, 2024.
- https://www.investopedia.com/articles/investing/091615/world-high-frequency-algorithmic-trading.asp •

Shamir, Boas. "Self Esteem and the Psychological Impact of Unemployment" *Social Psychology Quarterly*. Vol. 49:2 pp. 61-77, 1986.
- https://www.jstor.org/stable/2786857?origin=crossref •

SAMSHA. *Substance Use Disorders Recovery with a Focus on Employment*. Substance Abuse and Mental Health Services Administration. 2021.
- https://store.samhsa.gov/sites/default/files/pep21-pl-guide-6.pdf •

Sharif, Mirssa. "Too much free time may be almost as bad as too little." Press Release. American Psychological Association. September 8, 2021.
- https://www.apa.org/news/press/releases/2021/09/too-much-free-time •

Sanzenbacher, Geoffrey. "Did Welfare-to-Work Policy Actually Work?" Progress-less. June 23, 2023.
- https://progressless.org/2023/06/27/did-welfare-to-work-policy-actually-work/ •

Sharma, Rakesh. "Are Crypto's High Trading Volumes a Scam?" Investopedia, October 24, 2024.
- https://www.investopedia.com/news/are-cryptos-high-trading-volumes-scam/ •

Schulmeister, Stephen. "A General Financial Transaction Tax: A Short Cut of the Pros. the Cons and a Proposal. WIFO Working Papers." No. 344. Austrian Institute of Economic Research. Vienna. 2009.
- https://www.econstor.eu/bitstream/10419/128890/1/wp_344.pdf •

Sifma Research. "2023 Capital Markets Fact Book." July 2023.
- https://www.sifma.org/wp-content/uploads/2022/07/2023-SIFMA-Capital-Markets-Factbook.pdf •

Sohns, Taylor. "Real Estate Vs. Stock Investments – What's Better?" Nasdaq. January 5, 2024.
- https://www.nasdaq.com/articles/real-estate-vs.-stock-investments-whats-better# •

Statista-1 "Average yearly wages in the manufacturing sector in China." Statista. December 11, 2023.
- https://www.statista.com/statistics/743509/china-average-yearly-wages-in-manufacturing/ •

Statista-2."Number of Children by Age Group 2022." Statista. July 5.2024.
- https://www.statista.com/statistics/457786/number-of-children-in-the-us-by-age/ •

Statista-3. "Wealth Distribution in the United States First Quarter 2024." Statista. August 21, 2024.
- https://www.statista.com/statistics/203961/wealth-distribution-for-the-us/ •

Statista-4. "Alcohol tax revenue in the United States form 2000 to 2028." July 5, 2024.
- https://www.statista.com/statistics/248952/revenues-from-alcohol-tax-and-forecast-in-the-us/#: •

Statista-5. "Poverty rate in the United States in 2023. by race and ethnicity." September 16, 2024.
- https://www.statista.com/statistics/200476/us-poverty-rate-by-ethnic-group/#: •

Statista-6. "Percentage of median income spent on premium contribution and deductible by U.S. employees from 2008-2020." March 22, 2023.
- https://www.statista.com/statistics/631987/percent-of-income-spent-on-health-plan-by-us-employees/:
-

Statista-7. "Direct premiums written by the health insurance industry in the United States from 2011 to 2023." November 1, 2024
- https://www.statista.com/statistics/1276474/direct-premiums-written-health-insurance-usa/ •

Statista-8. "Bitcoin (BTC) 24 hour trade volume from July 1, 2020, to September 25, 2024." September 25, 2024
- https://www.statista.com/statistics/1272819/bitcoin-trade-volume// •

Statista-9. "Passenger Cars - United States." (Accessed 12/28/2024).
- https://www.statista.com/outlook/mmo/passenger-cars/united-states •

Statista-10. "Total out-of-pocket heath care payment in the United States from 1960 to 2022." January 10, 2024.
- https://www.statista.com/statistics/484568/us-total-out-of-pocket-health-care-payments-since-1960/s •

Tanner, Michael. "Poverty and Welfare." *Cato Handbook for Policy Makers*. Cato Institute. 2022.
- https://www.cato.org/cato-handbook-policymakers/cato-handbook-policymakers-9th-edition-2022/poverty-welfare •

Tax Policy Briefing Book. "How does the tax exclusion for employer-sponsored health insurance work?" January 2024.
- https://taxpolicycenter.org/briefing-book/how-does-tax-exclusion-employer-sponsored-health-insurance-work •

Tax Policy Center. "Key Elements of the U.S. Tax System." (Accessed 9/16/2024).
- https://www.taxpolicycenter.org/briefing-book/what-are-major-federal-excise-taxes-and-how-much-money-do-they-raise •

Tester, Jon. *Grounded: A Senator's Lessons on Winning Back Rural America*. New York: Ecco Press. 2020.

Timiraos, Nick. "Biden's Approach to Inflation Left a Big Opening for Trump." *Wall Street Journal*, November 19–2024.
- https://www.wsj.com/public/resources/documents/g4RyM5hGjaTHkihId2OG-WSJNewsPaper-11-19-2024.pdf •

Theiss. Eliza. "All You Need to Know About Real Estate Transfer Taxes by State in 2024." Property Shark. 2024.
- https://www.propertyshark.com/info/real-estate-transfer-taxes-by-state/ •

Thompson, Megan, et al. "State TANF Policies, A Graphical Overview of State TANF Policies as of July 2016." OPRE Report 2018-55. Office of Planning, Research, & Evaluation (OPRE), HHS Urban Institute. May 2018.
- https://www.urban.org/sites/default/files/publication/98780/state_tanf_policies_a_graphical_overview_of_state_tanf_policies_as_of_july_2016_1.pdf •

Toulvila, Alicia. "The Small Business Healthcare Tax Credit" Investopedia. April 30, 2024.
- https://www.investopedia.com/the-small-business-healthcare-tax-credit-5070476 •

Tolbert, J., et al. "The Uninsured Population and Health Coverage." *Health Policy 101*, KFF, May 28, 2024.
- https://www.kff.org/health-policy-101-the-uninsured-population-and-health-coverage/ •

Trading Economics. "United States - Stocks Traded, Total Value." January 2025.
- https://tradingeconomics.com/united-states/stocks-traded-total-value-us-dollar-wb-data.html •

US Customs and Boarder Protection. "Trade Statistics." September 19–2024.
- https://www.cbp.gov/newsroom/stats/trade •

US DOT. "Cruise Ship Port Calls and Passenger Counts." US Dept. of Transportation Bureau of Transportation Statistics. 2024.
• hhttps://data.bts.gov/stories/s/Cruise-Ship-Calls-and-Passenger-Counts/ucnj-kcz7/ •

US Energy Information Administration. "Tracking electricity consumption from U.S. cryptocurrency mining operations." February 1, 2024.
• https://www.eia.gov/todayinenergy/detail.php?id=61364 •

USA Facts-1. "How wealth distribution changed over time." USA Facts. November 13, 2023.
• https://usafacts.org/articles/how-has-wealth-distribution-in-the-us-changed-over-time/# •

USA Facts-2. "How is the American middle-class doing? What support does the government provide people?" USA Facts. 2023.

USDA. "Ag and Food Sectors and the Economy." USDA Economic Research. April 19–2024.
• https://www.ers.usda.gov/data-products/ag-and-food-statistics-charting-the-essentials/ag-and-food-sectors-and-the-economy/# •

Wager, Emma. et al. " How does health spending in the U.S. compare to other countries?" Peterson-KFF. January 23, 2024.
• https://www.healthsystemtracker.org/chart-collection/health-spending-u-s-compare-countries/ •

Vance, J. D. *Hillbilly Elegy*. New York: Harper. 2018.

Wandner, Stephen. *Transforming Unemployment Insurance for the Twenty-First Century: A Comprehensive Guide to Reform*. Kalamazoo, MI: Upjohn Press. 2023.

Varun, VM. "Prospects and Models of Combating Cryptocurrency Crimes." eucrim, issue 4. 2023.
• https://eucrim.eu/articles/prospects-and-models-of-combating-cryptocurrency-crimes/# •

Warren, Elizabeth, Ameia Warren Tyagi. *The Two Income Trap*. New York: Basic Books. 2003.

Waters. Emma. Owne Minott. Andrew Loutz. "Is it Time for Congress to Reconsider the Mortgage Interest Deduction?" Bipartisan Policy Center. November 2, 2023.
• https://bipartisanpolicy.org/explainer/is-it-time-for-congress-to-reconsider-the-mortgage-interest-deduction/ •

Weir, Matthew, et. al. "Billions in Tip-Related Tax Noncompliance Are Not Fully Addressed and Tip Agreement Are Generally Not Enforced." Ref # 2018-30-081. Treasury Inspector General for Tax Administration. September 28, 2018.
• https://www.oversight.gov/sites/default/files/oig-reports/201830081fr.pdf •

Wessel, David. "What is the Child Tax Credit? And how much is refundable?" Brookings. February 1, 2024.
• https://www.brookings.edu/articles/what-is-the-child-tax-credit-and-how-much-of-it-is-refundable/ •

Wiggin, Addison. "The Food Crisis of 2011." *Forbes*. April 21, 2021.
• https://www.forbes.com/sites/greatspeculations/2010/10/27/the-food-crisis-of-2011/ •

Wile, Rob. "Back In The Day. Brocker Got Away with Murder In Trading Commissions." *Business Insider*. May 31, 2014.
• https://www.businessinsider.com/historical-trading-commissions-2014-3 •

WorkCompLab. "Workers' Compensation by Industry" US Bureau of Labor Statistics." (Accessed 7/23/2024).
• https://workcomplab.com/insurance-industry/ •

World Bank Group. "Market capitalization of listed domestic companies (current US$) - United States 1975-2022. (Accessed 9/21/2024).
• https://data.worldbank.org/indicator/CM.MKT.LCAP.CD?locations=US •

World Population Review. "Healthiest Countries 2024." 2024.
• https://worldpopulationreview.com/country-rankings/healthiest-countries •

Worldometer. "GDP Per Capita". (Accessed 9/8/2024).
• https://www.worldometers.info/gdp/gdp-per-capita/ •

VA. "Budget." Veterans Administration. 2023.
• https://department.va.gov/administrations-and-offices/management/budget/ •

YCharts. "Bitcoin Transactions per Day." (Accessed 12/26/2024).
• https://ycharts.com/indicators/bitcoin_transactions_per_day •

Yun. Lawrence. et al. "Wealth Gains by Income And Racial/Ethnic Group." National Association of Realtors. April 2023.
• https://www.nar.realtor/sites/default/files/documents/2023-04-wealth-gains-by-income-and-racial-ethnic-group-04-18-2023.pdf •

Zhu Xiao Di. Eric Belsky. Xiaodong Liu. "Do homeowners achieve more household wealth in the long run?" *Journal of Housing Economics*. Vol. 16:3, 2007. Pages 274-290.
• https://doi.org/10.1016/j.jhe.2007.08.001. •

York, Erica, Taylor Cazy. "Summary of the Tax Credits Claimed on the Form 1040, Tax Year 2020." August 17, 2023.
• https://taxfoundation.org/data/all/federal/irs-form-1040-income-tax-credits/•

Zinn, Dori. "How to flip a house: A beginner's guide." Bankrate. July 8, 2024.
• https://www.bankrate.com/real-estate/flipping-houses/ •

INDEX

Symbols
$14 per hour wage 5, 34–35, 42, 44, 48, 50, 64–65, 67, 92–93
$30 per hour wage 5, 19, 35–36, 42, 44, 67, 92–93
16th Amendment 31

A
ACA (Affordable Care Act) 60, 62, 67–68
addiction 71, 89
affordable housing 41, 53
agriculture 35, 42, 67
AI (Artificial Intelligence) 80–82
  • AI-generated 82
airlines 15, 48, 93
alcohol 31, 48
American Unemployment and Temporary Disability Insurance 86
American Worker 2, 5, 7, 13, 20–21, 23, 27, 31–36, 41, 44–45, 51, 56, 59–60, 67, 76, 79, 82, 84–86, 88–89, 91–92, 94
  • employee 35, 40, 65, 67, 87–88
  • household budget 92
  • tax burden 34–35, 41, 92
  • UI (unemployment insurance) 93
  • unemployed 84
  • wage earner 34, 68
American Worker Tax Relief 42
automation 20, 81

B
balanced budget 91
barter 15
Biden, President Joe 91–92
bid-to-ask 37
biological markets 11
Bitcoin See cryptocurrency
Black American (African American) 15, 29, 72
Black Monday 29
bonds 24, 38, 39
brokerage fees 39
bubble 29, 55
business 2, 7, 13, 20–21, 23–25, 27–28, 31–37, 39–41, 54–55, 59, 69, 72–74, 77, 80–83, 87, 92. *See also* employer
businesses that employ 32, 34
business owner 13, 54

C
call centers 83
Canada 65
cannabis. *See* marijuana
capital 25
capital gain 25, 42
capitalism 12, 17, 21, 25
capitalist 17, 20, 24
capital leverage 34
cars 27, 48
Carville, James 11
case workers 76
CBO (Congressional Budget Office) 37–42, 48–50, 60–67, 69
child 7, 12–13, 34, 45–48, 50–51, 59, 62, 64, 66, 75, 93
Child and Dependent Care Tax Credit 46–48
childcare 5, 15–16, 45–46, 48–51, 70, 76, 92–93
  • parental childcare 15
Childcare cost 48–49
Childcare Trust 50
Child Sustenance 5, 46, 50, 76
Child Credit, tax 45, 47–48
China 12, 14, 31, 33–34, 80
Chinese worker 33
Chisholm, Shirley 72, 76
Clinton, President Bill 11, 91
cognitive disability 71
college degree 33
commercial insurance. *See* private health insurance
commodity 31, 38
companies that hire. *See* businesses that employ
company. *See* business

competition 25, 86
Congress 79, 82–84
Congressional Research Service 50
consumer spending 14, 92
copyright 82
COVID-19 65, 84–85, 91
craftsperson 19, 24–25
criminals 80
cruise ships 48–49
cryptocurrency 40, 79–80, 94
 • Bitcoin 40, 79

D

day-labor 8
day trading 28
deduction 40–41, 79
deficit, National 1, 91–92
derivative art 82
derivatives 28, 38–40
differential property tax 93
differential tax 56
disability 49, 63, 71, 85, 94
Disability Insurance 84, 86
DoD (Department of Defense) 63
DoD medical services 63–64
domestic abuse 75
down payment 54
drugs 88. *See also* addiction

E

economy 9, 11–14, 17, 23–25,
    27, 29, 31–33, 37–38, 44–45,
    80–81, 88, 91–92, 94
 • monetary economy 70
 • real economy 17, 27, 29, 33, 38,
    44–45, 80–81
        » real economy definition 13
empire model 17
employee. *See* American Worker
employer 5, 34–35–36, 44, 62, 65,
    67–68, 72, 84, 87–88
 • tax burden 34–35
employer-funded medical insurance
    62
energy 79–81
equal-pay-for-equal-value 16
equal-pay-for-equal-work 15–16
ETF (Exchange Traded Fund) 38, 40
Excess Wealth 23
excise tax 31, 48

exclusion for employer medical
    plans 67

F

FAA (Federal Aviation Administra-
    tion) 48
factory 20, 32, 55, 81. *See also* man-
    ufacturing
factory worker 35
family 79, 84, 86
farming 2, 7, 44, 80–81 *See also* ag-
    riculture
FCC (Federal Communications
    Commission) 83
federal tax 49, 92
financial instrument 37, 39–40
financial transactions 33, 38, 40, 93
    See also transaction tax
flat fee or flat tax 47, 67
flipping, house 54–55
food 13, 15, 39, 53, 72
food inflation 53
food preparation in the home 15
Ford, Henry 27, 32
Ford Motor Company 27, 32
Form 1040 79
Form I-9 87
full time 36, 48
futures 28

G

GDP (Gross Domestic Product)
    14–16–17, 31, 32, 59, 70
 • monetary GDP 15, 70
 • per capita GDP 14, 16
 • RDP (Real Domestic Product)
    14–15
 • Unmeasured Domestic Product
    15
generative AI 82
Germany 65
gig workers 35
Goldman Sachs 39
Great Depression 85, 91
Great Recession 85
Green Card 36
greenhouse gas tax 50

H

HDP (Household Domestic Product) 15
healthcare 5, 59–61, 63–70, 76, 92–93
- ACA (Affordable Care Act) 62, 67–68
- administrative efficiency 65
- DoD medical services 63–64
- healthcare cost 5, 59–60, 64–65, 93
- healthcare cost highest per capita 59, 64
- health insurance 66
- Indian Health Service 64
- LTSS (Long-term Services and Supports) 62
- Medicaid 62–63, 66, 76
- Medicare 34, 61–62, 66, 68, 89, 93
- National Health Plan 61–62, 64
- per capita healthcare costs 65
- single-payer 61–62

healthcare insurance 64, 66, 68
- employer-funded medical insurance 62
- Medicaid 60, 61–62, 63, 65–66, 76
- Medicare 34, 61–62, 66, 68, 89, 93
- Medicare-for-All 61, 69, 89, 93
- National Health Plan 59, 61–62, 64, 69
- preexisting conditions 60
- premium, healthcare 5, 59, 61–62
- private health insurance 61, 64, 69
- single-payer 61–62, 66, 69
- verterans administration healthcare 63–64

healthcare services 63–64, 69
Healthcare Trust 68
health coverage 76
health insurance *See* healthcare insurance
hedge 24, 39–40
Heritage Foundation 61
high-frequency trade 38
high-income 41, 47
high-tech 34
Hispanic 72
homeless 54, 71, 84
homeownership 41, 53
homestead 55

house flipping 55–56, 93
household 9, 16–17, 45–46, 79–81
- HDP (Household Domestic Product) 15
- household budget 2, 59, 92
- household economics 16, 33

household savings 92
housing 5, 13, 16, 41, 53, 55–56, 70, 73, 75, 92
- affordable housing 41, 53
- house, economic utility of 8, 16, 54–55
- housing prices 53
- long-term rental 56–57, 93
- primary residence 5, 53, 54, 56–57

humanist ethics 12

I

IA-generated. *See* generative AI
illegal immigrant 15, 50, 63–64, 86, 94. *See also* undocumented worker
income tax 5, 31, 34, 42
independent contractors 35–36
Indian Health Service 64
infant 46
inflation 24, 54
inheritance tax 42
innovation 25
institutionalized racial segregation and prejudice 72
insurance 84
Internet 72, 83
invest 14, 20, 25, 27–28, 35, 89
IRS (Internal Revenue Service) 15, 31, 36, 45, 48, 75, 87
itemized deductions 40–41, 43, 93

J

Jefferson, President Thomas 13
Johnson, President Lyndon B. 91
Judeo-Christian ethics 12

K

Keynesian 91

L

labor 7–8, 15–16, 21, 23–24, 31–35, 49, 83, 86–88

labor costs 34
labor-saving devices
laid off 84
legal resident 61–62, 83
Lincoln, President Abraham 31
liquidity 28
living wage 34
local government 55
long-term investment 28, 37, 93
long-term rentals 56–57, 93
low-income 41, 45, 84
LTSS (Long-term Services and Supports) 62–63, 66, 68

M

mansion 54
manufacturing 1, 2, 5, 11, 14, 31, 33–35, 42–44, 67, 92. *See also* factory
  • high-tech manufacturing 34
  • low-tech manufacturing 33
  • production line 27
manufacturing jobs 5, 31
manufacturing wage in China 33
manufacturing worker. *See* worker: factory worker
margin 28
marijuana 48
market crashes 38
market mechanism 69. *See also* competition
Marx, Karl 12
median home price 54
median income 16
Medicaid 60–66, 76
medical services. *See* healthcare services
Medicare 34, 60–62, 65–66, 68–69, 89, 93
Medicare-for-All 61, 89, 93. *See also* National Healthcare Program
Medicare tax 62, 68
mental health 73–74, 76, 89
mental illness 71–72, 89
mercantile 17
middle-class 86
mill 55
minimum wage 8, 36
monetary 14–16, 70
Montana 2, 34, 72–73, 75

mortgage 39, 41, 54
  • mortgage derivatives 39
  • mortgage interest 41
Musk, Elon 32

N

National Healthcare Premium 67, 69
National Healthcare Program 61, 67
National Health Plan 59, 61–62, 64, 69
National Health Program 70
National Heathcare 62
National Semiconductor Training Center 92
National Unemployment Insurance System 84
Native American 72
negative-sum 54
Nelson, Jaeger 62
net investment income tax 42
net zero tax impact 36
New Deal 91
New Jersey 85, 94
New York State 37
non-monetary 14–15
Nvidia 28

O

options, stock 28, 40 *See also* derivatives
option-to-buy 56

P

paid time 36
pandemic 65, 84–85, 91
P/E (price/earnings ratio) 24
per capita definition 14
personal income 35
phone number 83
poker 27, 80
pornographic 83
poverty 5, 45, 47, 63, 71–72, 75, 76, 94
preexisting conditions 60
premium, healthcare 59, 61–62, 65, 67–68
Premium Tax Credit 67
primary residence 5, 53–54, 56–57

private health insurance *See* health insurnace/private health insurance
private insurance 61, 69
productivity 14, 31–32, 70, 81, 89, 92
Profit 19, 24–25
profits 12, 24, 27, 42
property tax 41, 55–57, 93
pure speculation 25, 28–29, 36–38, 44, 54–55

R

Railroad Barons 13
RAND Corporation 62
Ravalli County, Montana 72–73
RDP (Real Domestic Product) 14–15
Reagan Administration 91
Reagan, President Ronald 91
Real Domestic Product 14
real economy 16–17, 27, 29, 33, 38, 44–45, 53, 56–57, 70, 80–81. *See* economy: real economy
real estate 54–55
real estate speculation 55
Real Labor Productivity 32
rental 56–57, 75
rentals 5, 56, 75, 93
retirement 8, 20, 25, 35, 68
Roosevelt, President Franklin Delano 91

S

savings 24, 44, 54, 64, 92
schools 55
S corporations 41
second homes 93
self-adjusting trusts 68
self-employment 9, 35
self-employment tax 35
server, computer 80
share 24–25, 41. *See also* stocks
share, stock 20, 24–25
short 55
short-term rentals 93
single parent 48
single-payer 61–62, 66, 69. *See also* Medicare-for-All, National Healthcare Program

single-payer cost 64–67
skewing the market 39
skilled worker 7
Smith, Adam 12
socialism 12–13, 17
social media 83
Social Security 5, 34, 42–44, 85, 87
speculation 25, 28–29, 36–38, 40, 44, 54–55, 93
 • day trading 28
 • house flipping 55–56, 93
 • margin 28
 • poop-and-scoop 28
 • pump-and-dump 28, 40
 • pure speculation 25, 28–29, 36, 37–38, 44, 54
 • short-squeeze 28
 • speculation, pure. *See* pure speculation
speculators 29, 37, 44, 54, 80
stockbrokers 37
stockholder 25, 54
stock market 25, 27–29, 39
stocks 20, 24–25, 27–29, 36–40, 54, 56, 93
 • stock certificates 20, 24
stock transactions 37, 93
supply-side 5, 91–92
Supreme Court 31
Switzerland 14, 65

T

tariff 34, 49, 84
tariff-free 49
tariff war 34
tax 5, 17, 28–29, 31, 33–49, 55–57, 62, 67–68, 70, 76, 79, 81, 87, 91–93
 • excise tax 31, 48
 • flat tax 67
 • income tax 5, 31, 34, 42, 46
 • Medicare tax 62, 68
 • mill 55
 • property tax 41, 55, 93
 • Social Security tax 5, 34, 42
 • tariff 34, 84
 • transaction tax 37–39, 43–44
 • transportation taxes 48
tax burden 17, 33–35, 41, 92
tax code 79
Tax Cuts and Jobs Act of 2017 41
Tax Free Worker Cost 40–41
tax-neutral 5, 36, 44
tax reform 3, 5, 31, 35–36, 44, 93

tech entrepreneur 7
terrorists 80
Tesla 28, 32
Tester, Jon 72, 76
T-Mobile 83
tobacco 48
Tracfone 83
transaction fee 37, 39. *See also* transaction tax
transaction tax 37–38, 39–40, 43–44
transfer tax 5, 37, 55–56, 93
transfer tax, short-term 56
Transforming Unemployment Insurance for the Twenty-First Century 84
treasury notes 38
trickle-down. *See* supply-side economics
trickle-up economics 70, 92, 94
Trump, President Donald 91
trust 36
 • Childcare Trust 50
 • Healthcare Trust 68
 • Social Security trusts 44
 • Worker Trust 42–44

U

Uber 36
UI (unemployment insurance) 15, 43, 84–86, 88
UK (United Kingdom) 65
undocumented worker 86, 88
unemployment 35, 43, 84–86, 93
Unemployment Insurance 35, 84, 93
uninsured 60, 66
Unmeasured Domestic Product 15
unpaid work inside the home 9, 13, 33, 47, 93
U.S. Flagged cruise ships 48–49

V

Value Added Tax (VAT) 79
Vance, J. D. 72, 76
VA (Veterans Administration) 49, 63–64
verterans administration healthcare 63–64
VoIP (Voice over Internet Protocol) 83–84
volatility 38
volunteer 15
vouchers, low income housing 5, 75
VPN (Virtual Private Network) 83

W

wage earner 34, 68
wait times (for healthcare) 61, 65, 69–70
Wandner, Stephen 84
wealth 17, 21, 23–25, 27, 29, 54–55
welfare to work 76
worker 5, 7, 20–21, 27, 32–35, 39, 41, 44–45, 67, 70, 76, 84–86 *See* American Worker; *See* Chinese worker
 • employee 35, 40, 65, 67, 73, 87–88
 • factory worker 32–33, 35
 • laborers 7
 • skilled worker 7
 • wage earners 23, 36, 92
Worker Trust 42–44, 68
workforce 34, 84, 86, 89, 94
working-class 7
workman's compensation 35, 63, 73, 84, 93
Work Permit 36
WPA (Works Progress Administration) 85–86

Y

Yellowstone TV series 72

Z

zero-sum 27, 38, 54–55

About the Author

James R. Olsen, Jim, is an engineer by trade, having successfully led large-scale, multi-company defense and air traffic control projects. He developed a double-bottom line business inspired by Patagonia. The company engaged in a variety of markets, delivering embedded teams into large projects, property management, and a native plant greenhouse operation. The company engaged with the community, for example, producing the Hamilton Performing Arts Series for a year to transition from the school district to a non-profit.

For the last 30 years, Jim has also been a volunteer grassroots activist engaged in forest and wilderness advocacy, effective domestic abuse intervention, local food systems, community-based mental health crisis management, subdivisions and water quality, and biosafety.

For the last ten years, Jim has focused on well-researched nonfiction books for the popular market. His writing hero is Erik Larson.

www.ingramcontent.com/pod-product-compliance
Lightning Source LLC
Chambersburg PA
CBHW061737070526
44585CB00024B/2717